Legal aspects of
develop

Rino Siffert
Ph.D., attorney-at-law and public notary, LL.M. (Cornell)
Certified Computer Scientist NDL

Siniša Petrović
Ph.D., tenured professor of law of the University of Zagreb

I

Foreword

In the world as globalized as it is nowadays, it is almost impossible to imagine an economy without foreign investments. A country's attitude towards foreign investment greatly differ; some have a more open-minded legislation and it really makes no difference whether an investment is domestic or from another country, while some countries tend to be more cautious and still perceive foreign investments as uncommon and treat them as an exception. Be it as it may for any reason, one basically cannot argue that foreign investments are not an important economic factor.

The content of this book is the result of the authors' professional experience from various capacities in which they dealt with foreign investments. The book is not intended to present an absolutely comprehensive research of all legal aspects of foreign investments; rather, it gives a general review of, in the authors' view, most important issues which either an investor or a host country may encounter. The purpose was to give a sort of checklist of these issues and to refer to legal sources, which help to find more detailed and profound answers to various problems that derive from foreign investments.

The intent of the authors was that the book can be used as a kind of textbook for introductory classes at law faculties, but also as a guide to legal practitioners and businesses. Even though most of the issues are notably important for investments in developing countries, we dare to say that many of them may be equally essential for any investment in any country, irrespective of its level of economic and legal development.

We are grateful mostly to the publishers for having being open to our basic idea of presenting the book to the public. The authors would also like to express gratitude to Dr. Tomislav Jakšić, assistant professor at the Faculty of Law University of Zagreb for his assistance in research and reading one of the earlier versions of the text.

Fribourg/Zagreb, February 2019

Table of contents

VII

Abbreviations

BIT	Bilateral Investment Treaty
BLT	Build, lease, transfer
BOOT	Build, operate, own, transfer
BOT	Build, operate, transfer
BT	Build, transfer
CISG	United Nations Convention on Contracts for the International Sale of Goods
cit.	cited/citation
COE	Communication on Engagement
Coface	Compagnie Française d'Assurance pour le Commerce Extérieur
COP	Communication on Progress
CSR	Corporate social responsibility
DOT	Develop, operate, transfer
e.g.	Exempli gratia/for example
ECGD	Export Credits Guarantee Department
ECT	Energy Charter Treaty
Et seq.	Et sequens/and the following
EU	European Union
FATF	Financial Action Task Force
G7	Groupe of Seven
GAFI	Groupe d'action financière
GATT	General Agreement on Tariffs and Trade
GRI	Global Reporting Initiative
i.e.	Id est/that is
IBRID	International Bank for Reconstruction and Development
ICC	International Chamber of Commerce
ICJ	International Court of Justice

ICSID	International Centre for Investment Disputes
IMF	International Monetary Fund
ISO	International Organization for Standardization
LCIA	London Court of Arbitration
MERCOSUR	Southern Common Market
MIGA	Multilateral Investment Guarantee Agency
MIT	Multilateral Investment Treaty
MOT	Modernize, operate, transfer
NAFTA	North American Free Trade Agreement
No.	Number
OAS	Organization of American States
OECD	Organisation for Economic Co-operation and Development
op. cit.	Opus citatum/work cited
OPIC	Overseas Private Investment Corporation
p./pp.	page/pages
ROT	Rehabilitate, operate, transfer
SCC	Stockholm Chamber of Commerce
TRIPS	Agreement on Trade-Related Aspects of Intellectual Property Rights
UN	United Nations
UNCAC	United Nations Convention against Corruption
UNCITRAL	United Nations Commission on International Trade Law
UNIDROIT	International Institute for the Unification of Private Law
USD	United States Dollar
VCLT	Vienna Convention on the Law of Treaties
Vol.	Volume
WTO	World Trade Organization

Literature

AHMED PRISCILLA A./FANG XINGHAI, Project finance in developing countries: IFC's lessons of experience (1999)

AHMED SAHID, Foreign direct investment, trade and economic growth: An introduction, in: Foreign direct investment, trade and economic growth, exploring challenges and opportunities, edited by Sahid Ahmed (2013)

AKEHURST MICHAEL, Custom as a source of international law, British Year Book of International Law (1976)

ALBANIA BUSINESS AND INVESTMENT OPPORTUNITIES YEARBOOK, Volume 1, Strategic, practical information and opportunities, (2016)

ALVAREZ JOSÉ ENRIQUE, The public international law regime governing international investment (2011)

ASOZU AMAZU A., International commercial arbitration and African States: practice, participation and institutional development (2001)

AUST ANTHONY, Modern treaty law and practice (2000)

BABU R. RAJESH, Remedies under the WTO legal system 2012)

BAETENS FREYA, Investment law within international law: integrationist perspectives (2013)

BAKER J. CRAIG, International law and international relations (2000)

BANKAS ERNEST K., The state immunity controversy in international law, private suits against sovereign states in domestic courts (2005)

BEGIC TAIDA, Applicable law in international investment disputes (2005)

BLAINE HARRISON G., Foreign direct investment (2009)

BORN GARY B., International commercial arbitration, volume 1 (2009)

BOULLE LAURENCE, The law of globalization: an introduction (2009)

BREAU SUSAN, Questions & answers, international law 2013 and 2014 (2013)

BUCKLEY PETER J./NEWBOULD GERALD D./ THURWELL JANE, Foreign direct investment by smaller UK firms: the success and failure of first-time investors abroad (1988)

BULJEVICH ESTEBAN C./PARK YOON S., Project financing and the international financial markets (1999)

BULT-SPIERING MIRJAM/DEWULF GEERT, Strategic issues in public-private partnerships, an internal perspective (2006)

BUMB BALU L., Privatization of agribusiness input markets, in: Privatization and deregulation, needed policy reforms for agribusiness development, edited by Surjit S. Sidhu/Mohinder S. Mudahar (1999)

BUTLER STUART, Privatization for public purposes, in: Privatization and its alternatives, edited by William T. Gromley, Jr. (1991)

CLAIRE CUTLER A., International commercial arbitration, transnational governance, and the new constitutionalism, in: International arbitration & global governance, Contending theories and evidence, edited by Walter Mattli/Thomas Dietz (2014)

COLLINS DAVID, An introduction of international investment law (2017) (cit. COLLINS, International investment law)

COLLINS DAVID, The BRIC states and outward foreign direct investment (2013) (cit. COLLINS, BRIC states)

COOK PAUL, Private sector development strategy in developing countries, in: Privatization and market development, global movements in public policy ideas, edited by Graeme Hodge (2006)

COUVREUR PHILIPPE, The international court of justice and the effectiveness of international law (2017)

DAHM GEORG/DELBRÜCK JOST/WOLFRUM RÜDIGER, Völkerrecht, volume I/3 (2013)

DAVISON MARK J./MONOTTI ANN L./WISEMAN LEANNE, Australian intellectual property law (2016)

DAWSON FRANK G./WESTON BURNS H., "Prompt, adequate and effective": a universal standard of compensation?, in: 30 Fordham L. Rev. (1962)

DE BRABANDERE ERIC, Investment treaty arbitration as public international law, procedural aspects and implications (2014) (cit. DE BRABANDERE, Investment treaty arbitration)

DE BRABANDERE ERIC, The settlement of investment disputes in the energy sector, in: Foreign investment in the energy sector, Balancing private and public interests, edited by Eric De Brabandere/Tarcisio Gazzini (2014) (cit. DE BRABANDERE, Settlement of investment disputes)

DERAINS YVES/SCHWARTZ ERIC A., A guide to the ICC rules of arbitration (2005)

DESSISLAV DOBREV, Reforming international investments laws: Is it time for a new international social contract to rebalance the investor-state regulatory dichotomy?, in: Yearbook on international investment law & policy 2014 – 2015, edited by Andrea K. Bjorklund (2016)

DIMATTEO LARRY A., International business law and the legal environment: a transactional approach (2017)

DINAVO JACQUES V., Privatization in developing countries, its impact on economic development and democracy (1995)

DIMSEY MARIEL, The resolution of international investment disputes, Challenges and solutions (2008)

DIXON MARTIN, Textbook on international law (2013)

DOLZER RUDOLPH/SCHREUER CHRISTOPH, Principles of international investment law (2012)

DUFFY JOHN W., Andean and Caribbean basin financing directory (1994)

DUGAN CHRISTOPHER F./ WALLACE, JR. DON/ RUBINS NOAH D./ SABAHI BORZU, Investor-state arbitration (2013) (cit. DUGAN/WALLACE, JR./RUBINS/SABAHI, Investor-state arbitration 2013)

DUGAN CHRISTOPHER F./WALLACE JR. DON/RUBINS NOAH D./ SABAHI BORZU, Investor-State arbitration (2011) (cit. DUGAN/WALLACE, JR./RUBINS/SABAHI, Investor-state arbitration 2011)

DUMOI AGUSMAN DAMOS, Treaties under Indonesian law: A comparative study (2014)

EGERTON-VERNON JAMES, Is investment treaty arbitration a mechanism to second-guess governments' exercise of administrative discretion: public law or lex investoria?, in: Investment treaty arbitration and international law, edited by Ian A. Laird, Borzu Sabahi/Frédéric G. Sourgens/Todd J. Weiler (2015)

EL-HOSSENY FAROUK, Civil society in investment treaty arbitration, status and prospects (2018)

ENDICOTT MARTIN, The definition of investment in ICSID arbitration: Development lessons for the WTO?, in: Sustainable development in world trade law, edited by Markus W. Gehring/Marie-Claire Cordon (2005)

FORD ALAN W., The Anglo-Iranian oil dispute of 1951-1952: a study of the role of law in the relations of states (1954)

FRIEDLAND PAUL D., Arbitration clauses for international contracts (2007)

GAZZINI TARCISIO, Interpretation of international investment treaties (2016)

GOOZNER MERRILL, The ten largest global business corruption cases, in: The Fiscal Times, December 13, 2011

GRAY CHRISTINE D., Judicial remedies in international law (1990)

GREENIDGE CARL B., Privatization in Ghana, in: Privatization, a global perspective, edited by V. V. Ramanadham (1993)

GUTTERMAN ALAN S., The law of domestic and international strategic alliances (1995)

GUTTERMANN ALAN S., A short course in international joint ventures, how to negotiate, establish and manage an international joint venture (2009) (cit. GUTTERMANN, International joint ventures)

HARDING MAEBH, Conflict of laws (2013)

HAREES LUKMAN, The mirage of dignity on the highways of humans 'progress': - the bystanders' perspective (2012)

HEPBURN JARROD, Domestic law in international investment arbitration (2017)

HIRSCH MOSHE, Interactions between investment and non-investment obligations, The Oxford handbook of international investment law, edited by Peter Muchlinski/Federico Ortino/Christoph Schreuer (2008)

HIRSCH MOSHE, Sources of international investment law, International investment law and soft law, edited by Andrea K. Bjorklund/August Reinisch (2012)

HOFFMANN SCOTT L., The law and business of international project finance: a resource for governments, sponsors, lenders, lawyers, and project participants (2001)

HOLLIS DUNCAN B., Sources in interpretation theories, in: The Oxford handbook on the sources of international law, edited by Jean D'Aspremont/Samantha Besson/Séverine Knuchel (2017)

HOLZER MARC/PRICE BYRON E./KANG HWANG-SUN, Public productivity handbook, edited by Marc Holzer/Seok-Hwan Lee (2004)

INKSTER IAN, Intellectual property, information and divergences in economic development – institutional patterns and outcomes circa 1421–2000, in: The role of intellectual property rights in biotechnology innovation, edited by David Castle (2009)

INTERNATIONAL LABOUR ORGANIZATION, sectoral activities programme, terms of employment and working conditions in health sector reforms, JMHSR/1998

INTERNATIONAL MONETARY FUND, Foreign private investment in developing countries (1985)

JACOBS VERNON K./FOX N. RICHARD, Risk management for amateur investors, A guide to higher yields with less risk for nonprofessional investors, plus an analysis of the impact of the new tax law on investors (2003)

JIMÉNEZ DE ARÉCHAGA EDUARDO, Interview: November 1993, in: Five Masters of International Law (2011)

JOHN KENNEDY M. MARIA, International economics (2014)

JOHNSTON R. BARRY/ÖTKER-ROBE İNCI, A modernized approach to managing the risks in cross-border capital movements, IMF Policy Working Paper No. 99/6 (1999)

JOYNER CHRISTOPHER C., International law in the 21st century, Rules for global governance (2005)

XVII

KJELDGAARD-PEDERSEN ASTRID, The international legal personality of the individual (2018)

KOJIMA KIYOSHI, Direct foreign investment, A Japanese model of multinational business operations (2010)

KRAYENBUEHL THOMAS E., Cross-border exposures and country risk: Assessment and Monitoring (2001)

KREUZER KARL F., Legal aspects of international joint ventures in agriculture (1990)

LEITE GUILHERME/ALVES RODRIGUES TALITA, Brazil, in: International joint ventures, the comparative law yearbook of international business, Special issue, edited by Dennis Campbell (2008)

LEPARD BRIAN D., Customary international law, a new theory with practical applications (2010)

LEW JULIAN D. M./MISTELIS LOUKAS A./KRÖLL STEFAN M., Comparative international commercial arbitration (2003)

LIM C. L./HO JEAN/PAPARINSKIS MARTINS, International investment law and arbitration (2018)

LINDBERG VAN, Intellectual property and open source: a practical guide to protecting code (2008)

LO CHANG-FA, Treaty interpretation under the Vienna Convention on the Law of Treaties (2017)

LOWENFELD ANDREAS F., International economic law (2002)

LUO YADONG, Multinational enterprises in emerging markets (2002)

MABABYA MAMARINTA P., The role of multinational companies in the Middle East: the case of Saudi Arabia (2002)

MAKONDO T., Privatisation as a major reform in public sector management, in: Public finance fundamentals, edited by Kabelo Moeti et al. (2007)

MCCORMICK MYLES/SHEPPARD DAVID, Egypt to pay Spanish-Italian JV $2bn in natural gas dispute, in: Financial Times, September 3, 2018

MCILWRATH MICHAEL/SAVAGE JOHN, International arbitration and mediation: A practical guide (2010)

MEINERS ROGER E./RINGLEB AL. H./EDWARDS FRANCES L., The legal environment of business (2018)

MERNA TONY/NJIRU CYRUS, Financing infrastructure projects (2002)

MILLER ROBERT/ GLEN JACK/JASPERSEN FRED/KARMOKOLIAS YANNIS, International joint ventures in developing countries, in: Finance & Development, March 1997

MODY ASHOKA, in: Infrastructure delivery: new ideas, big gains, no panaceas, in: Infrastructure delivery, private initiative and the public good, edited by Ashoka Mody (1996)

NADAKAVUKAREN SCHEFER KRISTA, International investment law, text, cases and materials (2016)

NAKAGAWA JUNJI, Nationalization, natural resources and international investment law, contractual relationship as a dynamic bargaining process (2018)

NDE FRU VALENTINE, The international law on foreign investments and host economies in Sub Saharan Africa, Cameroon, Nigeria, and Kenya (2010)

NEWCOMBE ANDREW/PARADELL LUÍS, Law and practice of investment treaties, standards of treatment (2009)

NG'AMBI SANGWANI PATRICK, Resource nationalism in international investment law (2016)

NIEMEYER RALPH T., Germany after capitalism (2012)

NIEUWENHUYS EVA/ BRUS MARCEL, Legal, political and economic aspects, in: Multilateral regulation of investment, edited by Eva Nieuwenhuys/Marcel Brus (2001)

NWOGUGU E. I., The legal problems of foreign investment in developing countries (1965)

OECD INTERNATIONAL INVESTMENT LAW, a changing landscape, a companion volume to international investment perspectives (2005)

OECD POLICY FRAMEWORK FOR INVESTMENT (2015)

OKEDIJI RUTH, New treaty development and harmonization of intellectual property law, in: Trading in knowledge, development perspectives on TRIPS, trade and sustainability, edited by Christophe Bellmann/Graham Dutfield/Ricardo Meléndez-Ortiz (2003)

ONWUAMAEGBU UCHEORA, International dispute settlement mechanisms – Choosing between institutionally supported and ad hoc; and between institutions, in: Arbitration under international investment agreements, a guide to the key issues, edited by Katia Yannaca-Small (2010)

ORAKHELASHVILI ALEXANDER, Peremptory norms and reparation for internationally wrongfully acts, in: Baltic Yearbook of international law, Volume 3, edited by Ineta Ziemle (2003)

ORTINO FEDERICO/ MERSADI TABARI NIMA, International dispute settlement: The settlement of investment disputes concerning natural resources – applicable law and standards of review, in: Research handbook on international law and natural resources, edited by Elisa Morgera/Kati Kulovesi (2016)

PARLETT KATE, Diplomatic protection and the International Court of Justice, in: The development of international law by the international court of justice, edited by Christian J. Tams/James Sloan (2013)

PETERS NIEK, The fundamentals of international commercial arbitration (2017)

PITEL STEPHEN G. A./RAFFERTY NICHOLAS, Conflict of laws (2010)

PRETORIUS FREDERICK/LEJOT PAUL/MCINNIS/ARTHUR ARNER DOUGLAS/FONG-CHUNG HSU BERRY, Project finance for construction and infrastructure, principles and case studies (2008)

PREVOT FRÉDÉRIC/MESCHI PIERRE-XAVIER, Evolution of an international joint venture: the case of a French – Brazilian joint venture, in: Thunderbird International Business Review, Vol. 48(3) (2006)

RASOULI GHAHROUDI MEHDI/HOSHINO YASUO/TURNBULL STEPHEN JOHN, Foreign direct investment, Ownership advantages, firm specific factors, survival and performance (2018)

RIPINSKY SERGEY/WILLIAMS KEVIN, Damages in international investment law (2008)

RUBINS NOAH, The notion of 'investment' in international investment arbitration, in: Arbitrating foreign investment disputes, procedural and substantive legal aspects, volume 19, edited by Norbert Horn (2004)

SABAHI BORZU, Compensation and restitution in investor-state arbitration, Principles and practice (2011)

SABAHI BORZU/BIRCH NICHOLAS J., Comparative compensation for expropriation, in: International investment law and comparative public law, edited by Stephan W. Schill (2010)

SALACUSE JESWALD W., The law of investment treatises (2009)

SALACUSE JESWALD W., The three laws of international investment: National, contractual, and international frameworks for foreign capital (2013) (cit. SALACUSE, The three laws of investment treatises)

SATTOROVA MAVLUDA, Reassertion of control and contracting parties' domestic law responses to investment treaty arbitration, between reform, reticence and resistance, in: Reassertion of control over the investment treaty regime, edited by Andreas Kulick (2017)

SCHAFFER RICHARD/AGUSTI FILIBERTO/DHOOGE LUCIEN J., International business law and its environment (2018)

SCHILL STEPHAN W., The backlash against investment arbitration, edited by Michael Waibel/Asha Kaushal/Kyo-Hwa Liz Chung/Claire Balchin (2010)

SCHMALENBACH KIRSTEN, Art. 26 Pacta sunt servanda, in: Vienna Convention on the Law of Treatises, A commentary, edited by Oliver Dörr/Kirsten Schmalenbach (2012)

SCHÖBENER BURKHARD/HERBST JOCHEN/PERKAMS MARKUS, Internationales Wirtschaftsrecht (2010)

SHAW MALCOLM N., International law (2017)

SMITH WARRICK, Covering political and regulatory risks: Issues and options for private infrastructure arrangements, in: Dealing with public risk in private infrastructure, edited by Timothy Irwin/Michael Klein/Guillermo E. Perry/Mateen Thobani (1997)

SORNARAJAH MUTHUCUMARASWAMY, Resistance and change in the international law on foreign investment (2015) (cit. SORNARAJAH, International law)

SORNARAJAH MUTHUCUMARASWAMY, The international law on foreign investment (2010) (cit. SORNARAJAH, Resistance)

STEWART DAVID P., Private international law, the rule of law and economic development, 56. Vill. L. Rev. 607 (2011)

TANG YI SHIN, The international trade policy for technology transfers: legal and economic dilemmas on multilateralism versus bilateralism (2009)

THIRLWAY HUGH, International law and its sources (2014)

TILMANN MICHAEL DRALLE, Ownership unbundling and related measures in the EU energy sector, Foundations, the impact of WTO law and investment protection (2018)

TOMUSCHAT CHRISTIAN, Individual reparation claims in instances of grave human rights violations: the position under general international law, in: State responsibility and the individual, edited by Albrecht Randelzhofer/Christian Tomuschat (1999)

TRAKMAN LEON E., Australia's rejection of investor-state arbitration: A sign of global change, in: Regionalism in international investment law, edited by Leon E. Trakman/Nicola W. Ranieri (2013)

TRAKMAN LEON E./RANIERI NICOLAS W., Foreign direct investment: a historical perspective, in: Regionalism inter international investment law, edited by Leon E. Trakman/Nicolas W. Ranieri (2013)

UNDP TANZANIA SUCCESS STORIES, FIGHTING CORRUPTION (2013)

UNITED NATIONS CONFERENCE ON TRADE AND DEVELOPMENT, Word investment report 2007, Transnational corporations, extractive industries and development (2007)

USMAN ADAMU KYUKA, Theory and practice of international economic law (2017)

VAN DE WALLE NICOLAS, Privatization in developing countries: a review of the issues, in: World Development, Vol. 17, No. 5 (1989)

VOON TANIA, The world trade organization, the TRIPS agreement and traditional knowledge: in: Indigenous intellectual property, a handbook of contemporary research, edited by Matthew (2015)

WANG GUIGUO, International investment law: a Chinese perspective (2015)

WARREN HEAD JOHN/FRISCH DAVID, Global business law: principles and practice of international commerce and investment (2007)

WILLMAN JOHN, Nationalisation: a blast from the past, in: Financial Times, January 18, 2018

WONG JARROD, Umbrella clauses in bilateral investment treaties: Of breaches of contract, treaty violations, and the divide between developing and developed countries in foreign investment disputes, 14 Geo. Mason L. Rev. 137 (2006)

WORLD DEVELOPMENT REPORT 1994, Infrastructure for development (1994)

YAN AIMIN / LUO YADONG, International joint ventures, theory and practice (2001)

YEN TRINH HAI, The interpretation of investment treaties (2014)

YOO JOHN/STRADNER IVANA, Customary law today, edited by Laurent Mayali/Pierre Mousseron (2018)

Legal aspects of foreign investments in developing countries

I. Foreign investments in developing countries and international law

1. Introduction

In an interdependent, globalized economy, investments and various transactions are often done across national borders. Cross border transactions of goods, services or resources happen between legal entities or private individuals of two or more nations. In this regard, *private international law* (*"conflict of laws"*) can play a major role as it is the legal framework composed of conventions, protocols, model laws, legal guides, uniform documents, case law, practice and customs that determines the applicable law.[1] The latter is a specific notion of private international law and refers to the national law that governs a given question in an international context. If a dispute arises over an international business transaction and there is not a choice-of-law clause in a contract, then a court will determine based on the private international law which of two or more conflicting domestic laws should govern the dispute.[2]

However, if there is a cross border investment or business transaction between a sovereign state and an individual or a legal entity of another state, then such dealings may also be subject to *public international law*. The latter is a body of rules that consists of conventions and international customs, which bind states *inter alia* in their relations with individuals or legal entities of another state, and is founded on certain underlying principles.[3] For example, states are sovereign in their own territory, every state possesses the capacity to enter into treaties or to conclude international conventions,

---

[1] DAVID P. STEWART, Private international law, the rule of law and economic development, 56. Vill. L. Rev. 607 (2011), pp. 607 et seq.

[2] See STEPHEN G. A. PITEL/NICHOLAS RAFFERTY, Conflict of laws (2010), p. 212 and 272; MAEBH HARDING, Conflict of laws (2013), pp. 141-142.

[3] RICHARD SCHAFFER/FILIBERTO AGUSTI/LUCIEN J. DHOOGE, International business law and its environment (2018), p. 30.

1

and no state has to submit to the laws of another (*"pari parim non habet imperium"*).[4]

International investment (protection) law is one of the most *dynamic areas of public international law*. There are many conventions and international customs, which define obligations.[5]

2. Sources of public international law

2.1. Generally

Article *38 of the Statute of the International Court of Justice (ICJ-Statute)*, which concentrates primarily on the activities of states, can be taken as a starting point for an overview of the four classic sources of public international law. This article is widely recognized as an exemplary statement of the aforesaid sources:[6]

> **Article 38 Statute of the International Court of Justice (ICJ-Statute)**
>
> The Court, whose function is to decide in accordance with international law such disputes as are submitted to it, shall apply:
>
> 1. international *conventions*, whether general or particular, establishing rules expressly recognized by the contesting states;

---

[4] JOHN WARREN HEAD/DAVID FRISCH, Global business law: principles and practice of international commerce and investment (2007), p. 563.

[5] FREYA BAETENS, Investment law within international law: integrationist perspectives (2013), p. xxvii.

[6] See HUGH THIRLWAY, International law and its sources (2014), p. 6; DUNCAN B. HOLLIS, Sources in interpretation theories, in: The Oxford handbook on the sources of international law, edited by Jean D'Aspremont/Samantha Besson/Séverine Knuchel (2017), p. 429 and MARTIN DIXON, Textbook on international law (2013), pp. 24-25. Article 38 ICJ-Statute does not contain a complete list of the sources of public international law (e.g., there is for example no reference to the UN resolutions).

2

2. international *custom*, as evidence of a general practice accepted as law;
3. the general *principles* of law recognized by civilized nations;
4. subject to the provisions of Article 59, *judicial decisions* and the *teachings of the most highly qualified publicists of the various nations*, as subsidiary means for the determination of rules of law.

2.2. Conventions

Article 38(1)(a) of the ICJ-Statute gives priority to *conventions* as a *major feature of international law*.[7] A convention is somehow similar to a contract of private law (where the parties are private persons, while here the parties are sovereign states), which also imposes obligations, and is therefore an international agreement concluded between states in writing, based on their consent to be bound by it and governed by international law. Such agreements are means of creating international rules or standards that states and other actors of the international community are supposed to abide by. These agreements are also referred to as treaties, charters, covenants, declarations, general acts, pacts and statutes, but regardless the various terminologies the substance is the same.[8] There are two types of conventions: (i) *bilateral conventions*, where only two contracting states are convention partners and bound by it, and (ii) *multilateral conventions*, where a lot of states are signatories and parties to the convention.[9] However, the national law of each signatory state stipulates how a state can become a convention partner. National (constitutional) law provides for the hierarchy of international agreements within the national legal system. In addition, depending on the national law, some act of a national legislation may be required for an international agreement to be given legal

---

7 THIRLWAY, op. cit., p. 7.
8 This is in line with basic legal principles like *"falsa nominatio non nocet"*.
9 See SCHAFFER/AUGUSTI/DHOOGE, op. cit., p. 30 and DIXON, op. cit., p. 28.

effect in the national legal system (e.g., ratification of an international agreement, i.e., its approval by the national parliament).[10]

Very often multilateral conventions allow the signatory states to make reservations or to opt out of certain provisions. Thus, it is possible that a state becomes a party of a convention without acceptation of every provision of it. However, there is a controversy whether a state can make a reservation or objection with regard to specific provisions of a convention if the latter does not offer such a possibility. Nevertheless, it is not possible to make unilaterally a reservation or an objection to a provision after a state has already signed a convention.[11]

As international investment conventions are part of the international law they need to be construed and applied with reference to general rules and concepts of international law. Therefore, it is often referred to the Vienna Convention on the Law of Treaties (VCLT) as its content is the guideline for interpreting and applying international conventions.[12] The latter governs the international law on treaties between states and as such it is a codification of customary international law.[13] The convention was adopted on May 22, 1969 and opened for signature on May 23, 1969. It entered into force on January 27, 1980 and up to now, 116 states have ratified it. For those states which have not ratified the VCLT, like the United States, the content of this convention is still of the nature of customary rules of international law and they are bound by such customary law.[14]

---

[10] The terms that describe a state's approach to the relationship between the national and international law are monism (national and international law make a unified legal system) and dualism (international agreements have to be transposed into national law). Many states have mixed systems, with some features of both monism and of dualism.

[11] See GEORG DAHM/JOST DELBRÜCK/RÜDIGER WOLFRUM, Völkerrecht, volume I/3 (2013), pp. 558 et seq.

[12] Article 31 VCLT; see also HOLLIS, op. cit., p. 429 and TARCISIO GAZZINI, Interpretation of international investment treaties (2016), pp. 56 et seq.

[13] See CHANG-FA LO, Treaty interpretation under the Vienna Convention on the Law of Treaties (2017), pp. 34 et seq.

[14] CHANG-FA LO, op. cit., p. 33 and DIXON, op. cit., p. 29.

Furthermore, it is noteworthy that there are many international agreements on trade and investment protections laws such as the WTO agreements, regional or bilateral free trade agreements and other treaties on economic integration (e.g., EU Treaties, NAFTA Agreement, MERCOSUR Agreement), treaties on investment protection like the ICSID-Convention, the Energy Charter Treaty (ECT), the Bretton Woods Agreement on the International Monetary Fund (IMF Statute) and the International Bank for Reconstruction and Development (IBRD).

2.3. International custom

Article 38(1)(b) of the ICJ-Statute mentions that international custom is also a source of public international law. In general, *customary international law* evolved from the consistent *practice or customs of states* is accepted as law.[15] State practices are any act or statement like physical acts, claims, declarations *in abstracto* (e.g., UN General Assembly Resolutions), national laws, national judgments and omissions.[16] It is agreed that the existence of a rule of customary international law requires the presence of two elements: (i) *state practice*, which is uniform, consistent and general (objective element) and (ii) *opinio juris* (subjective element), which is the belief that a practice is compulsory.[17] This is especially the case if a number of states follow the same practice. Furthermore, customary international law can

---

[15] See Dixon, op. cit., p. 32.

[16] J. Craig Baker, International law and international relations, (2000), pp. 56-57. and John Yoo/Ivana Stradner, Customary law today, edited by Laurent Mayali/Pierre Mousseron (2018), p. 320.

[17] E.g., ICJ, Reports of judgments, advisory opinions and orders, case concerning the continental shelf, North Sea continental shelf cases (Federal Republic of Germany/Denmark; Federal Republic of Germany/Netherlands), Judgment of February 20, 1969, pp. 38 et seq. or ICJ, Reports of judgments, advisory opinions and orders, case concerning the continental shelf (Libyan Arab Jamahiriya/Malta), Judgment of June 3, 1985, pp. 20-21.

also be created by the practice of international organizations and by the practice of individuals.[18]

In principle, customary international law steps behind specific rules or conventions. However, there is the exception of customary international law rising to the level of *jus cogens* through acceptance by the international community as non-derogable rights (e.g., elementary human rights). No derogation is ever allowed to *jus cogens* as these norms have their roots in natural law principles.[19]

There are various rules of customary international law that might be important in cross border transactions like state responsibility, state immunity and '*minimum standard*' for the treatment of foreign nationals.

2.4. General principles

Article 38(1)(c) of the ICJ-Statute lists the general principles of law recognized by civilized nations as one of the sources of public international law. They play a lesser role as they complement conventions and customary international law.[20] Essentially, they fill the gap if there is neither a provision in an international convention, nor a recognized customary principle of international law available in an investment dispute.[21] These general principles are considered – due to their level of generality – to be fundamental, as they are widely recognized by states and therefore are common to nearly all legal systems.[22] For example, the principle of good faith is one of these general principles.

---

[18] MICHAEL AKEHURST, Custom as a source of international law, British Year Book of International Law (1976), p. 11.

[19] See BRIAN D. LEPARD, Customary international law, a new theory with practical applications (2010), pp. 336-337.

[20] THIRLWAY, op. cit., p. 8.

[21] See JAMES EGERTON-VERNON, Is investment treaty arbitration a mechanism to second-guess governments' exercise of administrative discretion: public law or lex investoria?, in: Investment treaty arbitration and international law, edited by Ian A. Laird, Borzu Sabahi/Frédéric G. Sourgens/Todd J. Weiler (2015), p. 228.

[22] DIXON, op. cit., pp. 43-44.

2.5.   Judicial decisions

Article 38(1)(d) of the ICJ-Statute mentions with regard to judicial decisions that they are *"subsidiary means for the determination of the rules"*. However, although judicial decisions are supposed to be limited to the parties and the particular case, most courts strive to follow previous rulings (*stare decisis*) and on occasion make new international law.[23]

2.6.   Teachings of the most highly qualified publicists of the various nations

Article 38(1)(d) of the ICJ-Statute states that the *"teachings of the most highly qualified publicists of the various nations"* are also among the *"subsidiary means for the determination of the rules of law"*. Therefore, the opinions of publicists are on the same level as judicial decisions and thus also considered as subsidiary source of law.[24] However, the teachings of publicists are essential for making the provisions in conventions and creating customary international law as well as general principles of law.

3.   Historical background of foreign investment law

Up to the past century, oversea investments went to colonies. As the colonies were controlled by imperial states, there was very often no need to develop a comprehensive framework to protect the rights of the investors that were domiciled in the imperial state. However, if needed the traditional *principle of state responsibility* was applied when states were held responsible for breaches of their obligations under international public law with regard to cross border investments. In the de-colonization-period, which started mainly after the Second World War, the imperial states lost their colonies. The latter became independent and nationalizations became frequent. The purpose of

---

[23] LINDA A. MALONE, International law (2008), p. 26.
[24] THIRLWAY, op. cit., p. 8.

nationalizations was not only economic (to take ownership of previously private investments by foreign parties and transforming them into public assets of newly independent states), but also political (to show the political power and authority of new non-colonial legal orders). There was a pressure for alternatives. The imperial powers saw a need to create new rules in order to protect foreign investments[25] as domestic law was inadequate to protect such investments. In addition to this, there have been conflicts between the USA and Latin America as well as political developments in Eastern Europe, which also led to nationalizations. These events increased the worries that foreign investments were not appropriately protected. The limited influence of a single state, the complexity of economic relations, the fast-changing political situations in states and the activities of transnational companies have fostered the conclusion of conventions in order to create foreign investment laws, the creation of international organizations like the World Bank and other forms of intergovernmental cooperation. However, the principle of state responsibility, which was for a long time nearly the only way to protect investments abroad, has not been replaced and can still be pursued.

4. State responsibility

4.1. Generally

Under the principle of state responsibility, which is considered to be customary international law and a fundamental principle of public international law, states are generally responsible for breaches of their obligations under international law.[26] Thus, if a state is responsible for a violation of international public law (e.g., through a breach of an obligation in a treaty by a state or when a harm has been done to a foreign investor due to an expropriation),

---

[25] The first bilateral investment treaty was adopted in 1959 between Germany and Pakistan, entered into force in 1962 and is still in force (see http://investmentpolicyhub.unctad.org/IIA/treaty/1732).

[26] See Publications of the permanent court of international justice, Series A., No. 9, July 26, 1927, Case concerning the factory at Chorzów.

then it has to make reparations for such a violation (e.g., compensation for the loss of property). State responsibility covers not only unlawful acts or omissions committed directly by the state, by its member states or provinces, but also acts or omissions of agencies of the state or of individuals if their behavior can be attributed to the state. In such a case, the agency has to act in its official capacity or by authority from the state, respectively the individuals were acting on behalf of the state.[27] In disputes regarding foreign investments it is not easy to enforce the rights of an investor, who is either an individual or a legal entity, as it is not only required that international law must be violated, but also due to the concept of state responsibility, which stipulates that the state has to intervene on behalf of the investor. Still today, as a general rule, an individual has no standing before international tribunals. For example, only states may appear before the ICJ in proceedings. An individual always needs specific arrangements by way of specialized treaties setting up appropriate bodies of adjudication.[28]

Mavrommatis Palestine Concessions

Publications of the permanent Court of International Justice, File E.c. III, Docket V.I, Judgment No. 2, August 30, 1924

The case was brought against Great Britain by Greece, because of Great Britain's refusal to recognize, as the sovereign power in Palestine under a mandate assigned by the League of Nations, the contractual rights acquired by Mavrommatis, a Greek national, through agreements signed with the authorities of the Ottoman Empire, the former sovereign power in Palestine.

The ICJ held: *"...it is true that the dispute was at first between a private person and a State – i.e., between M. Mavrommatis and Great Britain. Subsequently, the Greek Government took up the case. The dispute then entered upon a new phase; it entered the domain of international law, and became a dispute between two States... It is an*

---

[27] See MALONE, op. cit., pp. 47-48.
[28] CHRISTIAN TOMUSCHAT, Individual reparation claims in instances of grave human rights violations: the position under general international law, in: State responsibility and the individual, edited by Albrecht Randelzhofer/Christian Tomuschat (1999), p. 14.

elementary principle of international law that a State is entitled to protect its subjects, when injured by acts contrary to international law committed by another State, from whom they have been unable to obtain satisfaction through the ordinary channels. By taking up the case of one of its subjects and by resorting to diplomatic action or international judicial proceedings on his behalf, a State is in reality asserting its own rights - its right to ensure, in the person of its subjects, respect for the rules of international law. The question, therefore, whether the present dispute originates in an injury to a private interest, which in point of fact is the case in many international disputes, is irrelevant from this standpoint. Once a State has taken up a case on behalf of one of its subjects before an international tribunal, in the eyes of the latter the State is sole claimant. The fact that Great Britain and Greece are the opposing Parties to the dispute arising out of the Mavrommatis concessions is sufficient to make it a dispute between two States within the meaning of Article 26 of the Palestine Mandate."

However, before a state can bring a claim to an international tribunal on behalf of an investor, international public law requires that there must be a *link* (e.g., nationality) between the state that starts the procedure and the investor.[29] Though, international public law generally does regulate the relationship between a state and its own citizens, but also holds a state responsible for mistreatment of a citizen of another state. The idea behind this is, that there is a difference between the way a foreigner and the way a citizen is treated. In fact, states have gone to the ICJ and sued other states based on things that have happened to their citizens. One thing that flows from state responsibility is that a state is entitled to diplomatic protection of its individuals.[30] However, opposed to these ideas is the so-called "*Calvo Doctrine*", named after the Argentine jurist Carlos Calvo, which has been applied throughout Latin America and other

---

[29] See International Court of Justice, Reports of Judgments, advisory opinions and orders, Nottebohm Case (Liechtenstein v. Guatemala), Second Phase, Judgement of April 6, 1955.
[30] See ASTRID KJELDGAARD-PEDERSEN, The international legal personality of the individual (2018), pp. 63-64.

areas of the world. This doctrine proposed to prohibit diplomatic protection of a foreigner as he has to be treated like a citizen and thus, he has to use local courts until *"local resources"* were exhausted.[31]

4.2. Individuals

Under international public law, a state may intervene only on behalf of individuals who are their citizens.[32] It is important that the state has a *sufficient link/genuine connection* to the individual before it can make a claim on behalf of the individual.

Nottebohm (Liechtenstein v. Guatemala)

International Court of Justice, Reports of Judgments, advisory opinions and orders, Nottebohm Case (Liechtenstein v. Guatemala), Second Phase, Judgment of April 6, 1955

The ICJ decided that Guatemala was not required to recognize the claim of Liechtenstein to represent Mr. Nottebohm, a naturalized Liechtenstein citizen, who had lived in Guatemala for years and who had very few ties to Liechtenstein, when Liechtenstein claimed that Guatemala had mistreated Mr. Nottebohm. The latter had insufficient links to Liechtenstein.

The term *'nationality'* was understood and defined by the ICJ as a *"legal bond having on its basis a social fact of attachment, a genuine connection of existence, interests and sentiments, together with the existence of reciprocal rights and duties. It may be said to constitute the juridical expression of the fact that the individual upon whom it is conferred, either directly by the law or as the result of an act of the authorities, is in fact more closely connected with the population of the State conferring nationality than with that of any other State. Conferred by a State, it only entitles that State to exercise protection vis-à-vis another State, if it*

---

31 EDUARDO JIMÉNEZ DE ARÉCHAGA, Interview: November 1993, in: Five Masters of International Law (2011), p. 107
32 See ASTRID KJELDGAARD-PEDERSEN, op. cit., pp. 63-64.

constitutes a translation into juridical terms of the individual's connection with the State which has made him its national."

4.3. Legal entities

A legal entity has the nationality of the state under the laws of which it was created or incorporated. However, it has been the practice of some states to give a legal entity, created or incorporated under their law, only diplomatic protection when it has its seat, management or center of control in their territory.[33] Thus, there must be a *sufficient link* between the legal entity and the state in order that the latter can bring forward a claim on behalf of the legal entity.

Barcelona Traction, Light and Power Company

International Court of Justice, Reports of Judgments, Advisory Opinions and Orders, Case Concerning The Barcelona Traction, Light and Power Company, Limited (New Application: 1962) (Belgium v. Spain), Second Phase, Judgment of February 5, 1970

The Barcelona Traction, Light and Power Co. was incorporated in 1911 under Canadian law for the purpose of supplying electricity in Spain. In 1938, Spain declared the company bankrupt and took other actions detrimental to it and its shareholders. Canada did not bring a suit in the ICJ, but, since an alleged 88 percent of the shareholders were Belgians, Belgium did. Spain objected that Belgium could not sponsor a complaint on behalf of Barcelona Traction's owners because only the corporation had been injured and the corporation was not Belgian.

The ICJ found that the injured party was the company and not its owners. Therefore, Belgium could not bring a suit to the ICJ against Spain on behalf of the company's Belgian owners. The ICJ noted that Spain had made no objection to

---

[33] KATE PARLETT, Diplomatic protection and the International Court of Justice, in: The development of international law by the international court of justice, edited by Christian J. Tams/James Sloan (2013), p. 99.

Canada bringing a complaint if it chose to do so: "*The Canadian Government's right of protection in respect of the Barcelona Traction company remains unaffected by the present proceedings. The Spanish Government has never challenged the Canadian nationality of the company, either in the diplomatic correspondence with the Canadian Government or before the Court. Moreover, it has unreservedly recognized Canada as the national State of Barcelona Traction in both written pleadings and oral statements made in the course of the present proceedings. Consequently, the Court considers that the Spanish Government has not questioned Canada's right to protect the company.*" Thus, only Canada would have been able to sue as the company was registered in Canada.

II. Definition of foreign investment and investment laws

1. Definition of foreign investment

1.1. Generally

A foreign investment can be defined as any transfer of capital, goods, technology, intellectual property, managerial skills and/or services by an individual or a legal entity of one state to the host state in order to generate wealth.[34]

Often national investment laws, conventions or investment contracts between an individual or a legal entity, which are acting as investors, and hosts states define in a very detailed way what a foreign investment is. The meaning is very important as it also describes when an investor can ask for protection of his investment or eventually a compensation from a host state for its acts.[35]

Foreign investments can be subdivided in *"foreign direct investment"* and a *"foreign portfolio investment"*.

1.2. Foreign direct investments

Foreign direct investments are investment which have been made in order to obtain a lasting interest in a legal entity, which is operating in a host state, and thus it is important for

---

[34] See VALENTINE NDE FRU, The international law on foreign investments and host economies in Sub Saharan Africa, Cameroon, Nigeria, and Kenya (2010), p. 14; KIYOSHI KOJIMA, Direct foreign investment, A Japanese model of multinational business operations, (2010), p. 134 and MUTHUCUMARASWAMY SORNARAJAH, The international law on foreign investment (2010), p. 8 (cit. SORNARAJAH, International law). Some authors argue that the widest definition of an *"investment"* in investment treaties can be found in the Energy Charter Treaty (Art. 1/6), see ERIC DE BRABANDERE, The Settlement of Investment Disputes in the Energy Sector, in: Foreign investment in the energy sector, Balancing private and public interests, edited by Eric De Brabandere/Tarcisio Gazzini (2014), p. 14.
[35] See also SORNARAJAH, International law, p. 10.

the investor to have the equity ownership, control over the operation, management policy and decisions. Generally, foreign direct investment include the formation of a subsidiary in the host state or an investor shareholding with voting rights of at least 10% in a foreign legal entity.[36] Moreover, control of technology, management, and crucial inputs can result in a *de facto control*.[37]

1.3.   Foreign portfolio investments

A portfolio investment is done by acquiring ownership of financial assets or participations in a legal entity incorporated or acting in another state without the same degree of direct control as in a foreign direct investment.[38] Usually they are short-term in nature.[39] These investments aim only to make profit and do not lead to technology transfer, to training of local cadres or a lasting interest in the investment or effective management control over a legal entity.[40] Portfolio investments involve a high turnover of securities; examples are debt certificates (money market securities, bonds), dividend-paying securities (shares, participation certificates, profit certificates) and mutual fund certificates.[41]

---

[36]   The voting rights should, generally speaking, give the investor some control over or of the object of the investment.

[37]   See HARRISON G. BLAINE, Foreign direct investment (2009), p. vii; MEHDI RASOULI GHAHROUDI/YASUO HOSHINO/STEPHEN JOHN TURNBULL, Foreign direct investment, Ownership advantages, firm specific factors, survival and performance (2018), pp. 1-2. and PETER J. BUCKLEY/GERALD D. NEWBOULD/JANE THURWELL, Foreign direct investment by smaller UK firms: the success and failure of first-time investors abroad (1988), p. 74.

[38]   See BLAINE, op. cit., p. 26.

[39]   GHAHROUDI/HOSHINO/TURNBULL, op. cit., p. 1.

[40]   NOAH RUBINS, The notion of 'investment' in international investment arbitration, in: Arbitrating foreign investment disputes, procedural and substantive legal aspects, volume 19, edited by Norbert Horn (2004), p. 317.

[41]   See MEHDI RASOULI GHAHROUDI/YASUO HOSHINO/STEPHEN JOHN TURNBULL, op. cit., p. 1.

1.4.   Distinction of the kind of investments

The distinction between these two different kinds of investments is not just theoretical as they are of practical importance. For example, ICSID does not provide protection regarding investment disputes about portfolio investments.[42]

> **Main elements for distinguishing foreign direct investments from foreign portfolio investments**
>
> *Ownership and control over the operation, management policy and decisions of the legal entity and share ownership:* A foreign portfolio investment is characterized by a separation between the control over the operation, management policy as well as the decisions and the ownership of the participations of the legal entity. Whereas in a foreign direct investment the investor wants also to have an effective voice in the management of the legal entity.
>
> *Long term aspect/withdraw of investment:* The investment of a foreign portfolio investor is of short-term in nature, he can easily withdraw his investment or transfer it to another investment. However, a foreign direct investment consists of a long-term commitment in which assets are bound and thus not easy to liquidate.

2.   Investments laws

2.1.   Generally

Foreign investments are important for the economic growth and prosperity of states. They are significant for any state, but for instance they have special meaning for developing countries. On one hand, they provide foreign investors with new markets and marketing channels, cheaper production facilities, access to new technology and products.[43] On the

---

[42]   See SORNARAJAH, International law, pp. 8-9.
[43]   SAHID AHMED, Foreign direct investment, trade and economic growth: An introduction, in: Foreign direct investment, trade and

other hand, the host state receives new capital, products, technologies and management skills.[44]

Thus, in order that foreign investments are made, there needs to be a legal investment protection, which is not only creating trust, but also reducing the risks of state interference.[45] Such risks derive *inter alia* from expropriation, restrictions on the transfer of assets, sanctions due to non-compliance with the domestic law, denial of permits, or other forms of unfair, inequitable, discriminatory or arbitrary treatment.

The law that applies to foreign investments consists of a complex bundle of (i) domestic investment legislation, (ii) investment treaties (bilateral and multilateral), and (iii) investment contracts between investors and states.

2.2.   Domestic investment legislation

In order to regulate, attract, promote or facilitate foreign investments, states usually issue *"investment laws"* or *"investment codes"* in their domestic law. In these investment legislations they offer a variety of guarantees, administrative services, tax incentives etc. However, also other fields in the landscape of law are of importance. Thus, the host states very often amend their commercial law, property law, labor law, civil procedure or criminal law in order to create a favorable environment for foreign investors.[46]

Moreover, certain countries generally allow investments only in the form of joint ventures and thus these countries have specific *"joint venture laws"*. A joint venture guarantees a host state to influence the management of a

---

economic growth, exploring challenges and opportunities, edited by Sahid Ahmed, (2013), p. 3.

[44]   See M. MARIA JOHN KENNEDY, International economics (2014), p. 293.

[45]   See OECD policy framework for investment (2015), p. 53.

[46]   See ALAN S. GUTTERMAN, The law of domestic and international strategic alliances (1995), p. 146 et seq. and MARIEL DIMSEY, The resolution of international investment disputes, Challenges and solutions (2008), p. 16.

legal entity, as local participants in the ownership and control of the investment project are involved.[47] Furthermore, a few states have enacted special investment laws that apply to particular sectors of the economy, such as agriculture, technology, tourism, services, or certain manufacturing areas, or their laws have been amended accordingly.[48]

2.3.   Investment treaties

In the last decades of the 20th century there was not only a striking increase in the flow of investments, but also the countries involved, the economic sectors concerned and the forms of investments evolved greatly.[49] The rise of foreign investments created a need for protection of the latter and investors against potentially 'unstable' legal systems of host states and thus led to an increase of investment treaties.[50] However, due to the influence of the aforementioned *"Calvo doctrine"*, which created *inter alia* a resistance towards the internationalization of investment protection, many countries in South America were initially not so keen in entering into investment treaties. Though, especially the United States bilateral treaty program with South America contributed to the demise of the *"Calvo doctrine"* in Latin America.[51] Nowadays, we count more than 2,500 investment

---

[47]   SORNARAJAH, International law, p. 107.
[48]   See ALAN S. GUTTERMAN, A short course in international joint ventures, Negotiating, forming and operating the international joint venture (2002), pp. 90-91.
[49]   MARTIN ENDICOTT, The definition of investment in ICSID Arbitration: Development lessons for the WTO?, in: Sustainable development in world trade law, edited by Markus W. Gehring/Marie-Claire Cordon (2005), p. 409.
[50]   DIMSEY, op. cit., p. 14.
[51]   MAVLUDA SATTOROVA, Reassertion of control and contracting parties' domestic law responses to investment treaty arbitration, between reform, reticence and resistance, in: Reassertion of control over the investment treaty regime, edited by Andreas Kulick (2017), p. 53 and CHRIOPHER F. DUGAN/DON, WALLACE, JR./NOAH D. RUBINS/BORZU SABAHI, Investor-State arbitration (2011), p. 69.

treaties, of which two-thirds were concluded in the 1990s.[52] Investment treaties have either the form of bilateral investment or multilateral investment conventions (*"BITs"* and *"MITs"*). The latter have been mainly concluded on a regional and interregional level. These treaties serve as a major vehicle for the protection of foreign investment interests of investors and their home states, but they were also created in order to promote foreign investment.[53]

Most investment treaties are concluded between developed and developing states at the developed state's request. Though, these investment conventions are supposed to be reciprocal, the protection is usually for the benefit of the developed states as the investments are made by its investors. Therefore, the treaty outcome does not always seem to be fair and there is often an inequity stipulated in the treaty. Event though, article 51 of the VCLT provides that where a state's consent to a treaty has been procured by coercion of its representatives through acts or threats directed against them, the treaty will have no legal effect, and article 52 VCLT states that the consequence is the same where threat or force has procured agreement to a treaty, there is no acceptance in international law that the mere economic pressure to enter in a treaty constitutes grounds for invalidating the agreement. Moreover, developing countries are not invoking these principles not just because they have no real evidence on this point, but also because they frequently lack the resources required to do so and they fear economic reprisals. However, an unfair behavior does not affect the validity of investment treaties under public international law.[54] On the other hand, it may be argued that an investment that was not made in accordance with the

---

[52] BURKHARD SCHÖBENER/JOCHEN HERBST/MARKUS PERKAMS, Internationales Wirtschaftsrecht (2010), p. 247 and DIMSEY, op. cit., p. 14.

[53] EVA NIEUWENHUYS/MARCEL BRUS, Legal, political and economic aspects, in: Multilateral regulation of investment, edited by Eva Nieuwenhuys/Marcel Brus (2001), p. 4.

[54] See LAURENCE BOULLE, The law of globalization: an introduction (2009), p. 144.

laws of the host state or international law is not protected by the investment legislation in general.[55]

Nevertheless, also some investment treaties were concluded between developing countries.[56] Furthermore, the investment treaties do not only set out the rules for foreign investments, but they are also a very important instrument in terms of creating a favorable investment environment, improved productivity and international competitiveness.[57]

Although it is difficult to make – besides the fact that these BITs and MITs promote investment and protect the interests of foreign investors from actions or omissions of the host state – general statements about the content of investment treaties, the latter usually grant investments made by an investor of one contracting state in the territory of the other the following guarantees:[58]

– Obligation of the host state to treat investors according to so-called *"minimum international standards"*;[59]
– Rights of investors to freely transfer currency out of the host state;[60]
– Right of the host state to expropriate assets of the investor located in the host state, with a corresponding duty to provide compensation;[61] and

---

[55] RUDOLPH DOLZER/CHRISTOPH SCHREUER, Principles of international investment law (2012), pp. 92-93.
[56] DIMSEY, op. cit., p. 13 and ANDREAS F. LOWENFELD, International economic law (2002), p. 456.
[57] INTERNATIONAL MONETARY FUND, Foreign private investment in developing countries (1985), p. 11.
[58] See DIMSEY, op. cit., p. 14.
[59] DESSISLAV DOBREV, Reforming international investments laws: Is it time for a new international social contract to rebalance the investor-state regulatory dichotomy?, in: Yearbook on international investment law & policy 2014 – 2015, edited by Andrea K. Bjorklund (2016), p. 275.
[60] JESWALD W. SALACUSE, The law of investment treatises (2009), p. 264.
[61] TILMANN MICHAEL DRALLE, Ownership unbundling and related measures in the EU energy sector, Foundations, the impact of WTO law and investment protection (2018), p. 238 and YI SHIN TANG, The international trade policy for technology transfers: legal and economic dilemmas on multilateralism versus bilateralism (2009), p. 84.

- Settlement of disputes between investors and the host state through international arbitration.[62]

Especially developed states, which are very active in negotiating investment conventions like the United States or Canada, usually have a boiler plate *"model treaty"* that is used as a starting basis for their negotiations with developing countries. Furthermore, many of the provisions in these *"model treaties"* are based on rules of customary international law.[63]

Nonetheless, in an investment dispute it might be necessary to have a close look at the validity of a certain provision in an investment treaty (e.g., if its content is in conflict with customary international law). Thus, it has to be distinguished whether the provision is an ordinary regulation or it is in contradiction with *jus cogens*. Art. 53 VCLT states that a provision in a treaty that contradicts *jus cogens* is void. The superior normative state of *jus cogens* rules has also been confirmed in several investment awards.[64] Even though there are states like the United States, which are not party to the VCLT, the previously mentioned rule applies as it is considered as customary international law.

---

[62] LOWENFELD, op. cit., p. 456 and DIMSEY, op. cit., p. 14.
[63] See LEON E. TRAKMAN/NICOLAS W. RANIERI, Foreign direct investment: a historical perspective, in: Regionalism inter international investment law, edited by Leon E. Trakman/Nicolas W. Ranieri (2013), p. 20.
[64] See MOSHE HIRSCH, Sources of international investment law, International investment law and soft law, edited by Andrea K. Bjorklund/August Reinisch (2012), p. 33 and MOSHE HIRSCH, Interactions between investment and non-investment obligations, The Oxford handbook of international investment law, edited by Peter Muchlinski/Federico Ortino/Christoph Schreuer (2008), p. 157. An example for such an investment award is the following: Corn Products International, Inc. v. United Mexican States, ICSID Case No. ARB (AF)/04/01, para. 149.

3. Investment contracts between investors and states

3.1. Generally

An investor may enter into an investment contract with the host state. There are varieties of such contracts, and their subject can be very wide. For example, such contracts are made frequently with regard to the extraction of natural resources (e.g., exploration and exploitation of oil, gas and minerals).[65] These contracts were made in order to protect the investors of unilateral changes by the host state (e.g., due to changes in the domestic law), which affect negatively the investors interests. However, a state's powers within its borders are not limitless under international public law. A host state is usually bound for promises it made to the investor. Therefore, a breach of such an investment contract is also a breach of international law.

Usually, under the principle of state responsibility investors have no legal personality on the international level; they might have to ask their home states to go forward for them in order to assert their claims. Nevertheless, investors have moved away from the simple diplomatic protection thanks to contractual stipulations in internationalized investment contracts between investors and the host state or BITs or MITs according to which they were able to enforce directly their rights before international tribunals or arbitration and thus they acquired partial legal personality under international law.

3.2. Investor-state contracts

A contract between a foreign investor and a host state binds the state under international law when it is *"internationalized"*. Such *"internationalization"* of an investor-state-contract occurs when the contract integrates

---

[65] See FEDERICO ORTINO/NIMA MERSADI TABARI, International dispute settlement: The settlement of investment disputes concerning natural resources – applicable law and standards of review, in: Research handbook on international law and natural resources, edited by Elisa Morgera/Kati Kulovesi (2016), p. 515.

international standards into the applicable law of their contractual relations by referring to customary international law or to BITs or MITs, which are ratified by their home or host states.[66] For example, the investor is granted by the host state a compensation and a fair and equitable treatment. Furthermore, the parties agree that to the extent that law of the host state governs the contract, it will not be unilaterally modified by the host state. Once a contract is *"internationalized"*, a state is responsible under international law for a breach of the contract. Furthermore, the effect of *"internationalization"* of contracts has been affirmed by international tribunals.[67]

Internationalization is accomplished by the inclusion of an (i) international choice-of-law clause and/or a (ii) *"stabilization clause"* in the investor-state agreement.

3.2.1. International-choice-of-law clause

An international-choice-of-law-clause[68] states that the international law will govern the contractual relationship between the parties and the principles of international law will be applied. The purpose of this type of clause is to *"internationalize"* the contract and thus protect it from attempts by the host state to cancel or modify it without the consent of the investor.[69]

Example of an international-choice-of-law-clause

The contractual relationship is governed by the principles of law of [state] common to the principles of international law and in the absence of such common principles then by and

---

[66] See MUTHUCUMARASWAMY SORNARAJAH, Resistance and change in the international law on foreign investment (2015), pp. 78 et seq. (cit. SORNARAJAH, Resistance).

[67] See JESWALD W. SALACUSE, The three law of international investment: National, contractual, and international frameworks for foreign capital (2013), p. 390 (cit. SALACUSE, The three laws of international investment).

[68] An international-choice-of-law-clause is not the same as a *"classical"* choice-of-law-clause, which refers solely to the law of a particular jurisdiction.

[69] SALACUSE, The three laws of international investment, p. 319.

in accordance with the general principles of law, including such of those principles as may have been applied by international tribunals.

Texaco Overseas Petroleum Company v. The Government of the Libyan Arab Republic

(1977) 53 ILR 389

In this case the tribunal held that one effect of an internationalization of a contract is that the individuals acquire and can enforce certain rights against the state: *"...stating that a contract between a State and a private person falls within the international legal order means that for the purposes of interpretation and performance of the contract, it should be recognized that a private contracting party has specific international capacities. But, unlike a State, the private person has only a limited capacity and his quality as a subject of international law does enable him only to invoke, in the field of international law, the rights which derive from the contract. ... The application of the principles of Libyan law does not have the effect of ruling out the application of the principles of international law, but quite the contrary: it simply requires us to combine the two in verifying the conformity of the first with the second."*

3.2.2. Stabilization clause

The stabilization clause states that between the parties of an investor-state-contract, the law of the host state as of the date of the contract or such other date agreed to by the parties governs the contractual relationship. The parties make sure that the applicable law on their contractual relations is safe from subsequent changes of the domestic law. The stabilization clause literally *"freezes"* the applicable law.[70]

---

[70] SORNARAJAH, Resistance, p. 110.

AGIP S.p.A. v. People's Republic of the Congo
ICSID Case No. ARB/77/71
In 1962, AGIP set up a legal entity under the law of the
Republic of Congo for oil distribution activities. The legal
entity was exempted from the nationalizations in 1974.
Art. 11 of the agreement contained a stabilization clause:
*"... adopt appropriate measures to prevent the application
to the Company of future amendments to company law
affecting the structure and composition of Company
bodies..."*

3.3. Investors rights under investment conventions

Modern BITs and MITs grant to an investor the right to sue
a host state directly in international arbitration, if he believes
that the BIT or MIT governing his investment has been
violated (e.g., Energy Charter Treaty).[71] The ability for a
foreign national or legal entity to sue a host state directly has
been described as a revolutionary innovation that has caused
a profound transformation of international public law.[72] For
such a right to sue the state directly in an international
arbitration by the foreign investor, a specific consent has to
be given in the convention.[73]

4. Binding effect of investor-state contracts and investment treaties

As states can enter into contracts and treaties and convey
special rights to investors, there is also the risk that the same
states take away these special rights. However, once a state

---

[71] SCHÖBENER/HERBST/PERKAMS, op. cit., p. 248.
[72] See A. CLAIRE CUTLER, International commercial arbitration,
transnational governance, and the new constitutionalism, in:
International arbitration & global governance, Contending theories
and evidence, edited by Walter Mattli/Thomas Dietz (2014), p. 145
and TRINH HAI YEN, The interpretation of investment treaties
(2014), p. 168.
[73] ERIC DE BRABANDERE, Investment treaty arbitration as public
international law, procedural aspects and implications (2014), p. 59.

entered into investment contracts and treaties, it is bound to respect its consent expressed in these agreements.

Article 26 VCLT "Pacta sunt servanda"

"Every treaty in force is binding upon the parties to it and must be performed by them in good faith."

The rule *"pacta sunt servanda"* is part of customary international law and a fundamental principle which dates back to early civilizations and became more and more important with the development of international law.[74] It does not only apply to conventions between states, but also governs contracts between investors and states.[75]

Sapphire International Petroleum Limited v. National Iranian Oil Company-Case

Sapphire Award, ILR 1963, at 136 et seq.

According to the arbitrators, it has been duly established that one party deliberately refused to carry out certain of its obligations and that this failure is a breach of contract: *"Moreover, it is a fundamental principle of law, which is constantly being proclaimed by international courts, that contractual undertakings must be respected. The rule pacta sunt servanda is the basis of every contractual relationship. Moreover, it is contained in the laws of both parties to the dispute..."*

For example, if a state enters into a contract with an investor of another state, and then breaches the agreement because of changes in the domestic law, there is not only a violation of the contract, but this is also a breach of public international law.

Final ICC Award No. 5485, YCA 1989, at 156 et seq.

According to the arbitrators, a specific article of an agreement was clear and had to be applied literally:

---

[74] See KIRSTEN SCHMALENBACH, Art. 26 Pacta sunt servanda, in: Vienna Convention on the Law of Treatises, A commentary, edited by Oliver Dörr/Kirsten Schmalenbach (2012) p. 436.

[75] SALACUSE, The three laws of international investment, p. 319.

> *"Whereas the rule pacta sunt servanda implies that the contract is the law of the parties, agreed to by them for the regulation of their legal relationship, and generates not only the obligation of each party to a contract to fulfill its promises, but also the obligation to perform them in good faith, to compensate for the damage caused to the other party by their non-fulfillment and to not terminate the contract unilaterally except as provided for in the contract."*

However, there is a risk that a state might try to justify its acts by invoking another principle of public international law that is called *"clausula rebus sic stantibus"*, which allows to terminate an agreement due to a change of circumstances after the conclusion of a contract.

Article 62 VCLT "Fundamental change of circumstances"

"1. A fundamental change of circumstances which has occurred with regard to those existing at the time of the conclusion of a treaty, and which was not foreseen by the parties, may not be invoked as a ground for terminating or withdrawing from the treaty unless:

(a) the existence of those circumstances constituted an essential basis of the consent of the parties to be bound by the treaty; and

(b) the effect of the change is radically to transform the extent of obligations still to be performed under the treaty.

2. A fundamental change of circumstances may not be invoked as a ground for terminating or withdrawing from a treaty:

(a) if the treaty establishes a boundary; or

(b) if the fundamental change is the result of a breach by the party invoking it either of an obligation under the treaty or of any other international obligation owed to any other party to the treaty.

3. If, under the foregoing paragraphs, a party may invoke a fundamental change of circumstances as a ground for terminating or withdrawing from a treaty it may also

invoke the change as a ground for suspending the operation of the treaty."

In order that the principle *"clausula rebus sic stantibus"* has priority over the principle *"pacta sunt servanda"*, the change in circumstance has to be fundamental in order to be sufficient to disrespect a contractual relationship.

Fisheries Jurisdiction

(United Kingdom of Great Britain and Northern Ireland v. Iceland)

I.C.J., 1973 I.C.J. 3

In this case the ICJ stated that *"... the changes of circumstances which must be regarded as fundamental or vital are those which imperil the existence or vital development of one of the parties."*

Although, parties have often invoked the principle *"clausula rebus sic stantibus"* before the ICJ or other tribunals, the latter mostly refused to apply this principle.

III. Remedies in case of violation of public international law

1. Generally

Due to the principle that no state has to submit to the laws of another ("*pari parim non habet imperium*"), an investor will be faced with problems of the *sovereign immunity (state immunity)* of the host state. Sovereign immunity is a principle of customary international law, by virtue of which a sovereign state cannot be sued before the courts of another sovereign state without its consent and thus is exempt from the jurisdiction of foreign national courts.[76]

> **The Schooner Exchange v. McFaddon**
> **11. U.S. 116, 137 (1812)**
> The U.S. Supreme Court stated: *"The full and absolute territorial jurisdiction being alike the attribute of every sovereignty and being incapable of conferring extraterritorial power, does not contemplate foreign sovereigns, nor their sovereign rights as its objects. One sovereign can be supposed to enter a foreign territory only under an express license or in the confidence that the immunities belonging to his independent, sovereign station, though not expressly stipulated, are reserved by implication and will be extended to him."*

Until the mid of the twentieth century, there has been mutual respect for the independence, legal equality, and dignity of all states. Thus, there was an *"absolute immunity"*. However, as states entered more and more in trading and various commercial activities, it became clear that such a strict immunity deprived for example investors that entered with a state in such activities of their remedies. Thus, the doctrine of *"restrictive immunity"* was created. According to this doctrine, a state cannot claim sovereign immunity if a lawsuit is based on its commercial activities. Therefore, it is important to distinguish between *"acta jure imperii"*, which

---

[76] STEPHAN W. SCHILL, The backlash against investment arbitration, edited by Michael Waibel/Asha Kaushal/Kyo-Hwa Liz Chung/ Claire Balchin (2010), p. 34.

are sovereign and also public acts of a state that are usually exempt from assessment or damages awarded by a tribunal of another state, and *"acta jure gestionis"*, which refer to commercial acts for which states cannot claim to be immune in front of the tribunal. However, it is sometimes quite difficult to distinguish these kind of acts.[77]

> **Re Canada Labour Code**
> [1992] 2 SCR 50, 1992 CanLII 54 (SCC)
> The Supreme Court of Canada stated: *"Historically, nation states enjoyed an absolute immunity from adjudication by foreign courts. Under international law, it was accepted that sovereign states should not be "embarrassed" by subjection to the control of a foreign judiciary. Over time, however, as governments increasingly entered into the commercial arena, the doctrine of absolute immunity was viewed as an unfair shield for commercial traders operating under the umbrella of state ownership or control. The common law responded by developing a new theory of restrictive immunity. Under this approach, courts extended immunity only to acts jure imperii, and not to acts jure gestionis."*

2. Remedies available to the state

2.1. Generally

If the acts of a state violate public international law (e.g., expropriation of the property of an investor without compensation by the host state), then the state becomes responsible to another state and the injured state can rely on the following remedies:

---

[77] ERNEST K. BANKAS, The state immunity controversy in international law, private suits against sovereign states in domestic courts (2005), p. 74.

30

- Remedies under customary international law like state responsibility[78] and/or
- Remedies set forth in international investment treaties.[79]

Chorzów Factory

Factory at Chorzow (Germ. v. Pol.), Series A.-No. 17, September 13, 1928, Collection of Judgments, No. 13, Case concerning the factory at Chorzów

In this case the ICJ stated that: *"The essential principle contained in the actual notion of an illegal act – a principle which seems to be established by international practice and in particular by the decisions of arbitral tribunals – is that reparation must, as far as possible, wipe out all the consequences of the illegal act and reestablish the situation which would, in all probability, have existed if that act had not been committed. Restitution in kind, or, if this is not possible, payment of a sum corresponding to the value which a restitution in kind would bear; the award, if need be, of damages for loss sustained which would not be covered by restitution in kind or payment in place of it-such are the principles which should serve to determine the amount of compensation due for an act contrary to international law."*

The aforementioned excerpt describes that a state may demand reparation for a wrongful act by the host state in order to wipe out all the consequences of the illegal act.

Reparations in the form of restitution in kind and compensation are predominant in public international law.

2.2. Restitution in kind

The host state has to recover as a restitution in kind (*"restitutio in integrum"*) any losses by the return of the same or new goods to the other state. Thus, the injured state is entitled to obtain from the state, which has committed an

---

[78] See R. RAJESH BABU, Remedies under the WTO legal system 2012), pp. 52 et seq. and CHRISTINE D. GRAY, Judicial remedies in international law (1990), p. 210.
[79] See DE BRABANDERE, op. cit., p. 65.

act according to public international law, the re-establishment of the situation that existed before the wrongful act was committed. However, it is possible to combine the restitution in kind with other remedies.[80]

Temple of Preah Vihear

Reports of Judgments, Advisory opinions and orders, Case concerning the temple of Preah Vihear (Cambodia v. Thailand), Merits, Judgment of June 15, 1962

In 1904, Siam and the French colonial authorities ruling Cambodia formed a joint commission to demarcate their mutual border mainly by following the watershed line of the Dângrêk mountain range, which placed nearly all of the Preah Vihear temple on Thailand's side. The border's location was depicted on a map in 1907 by French officers on which the Preah Vihear area and its temple was placed on the Cambodian side. This map was sent to the Siamese authorities and used in the ruling of the ICJ. After the withdrawal of French troops from Cambodia in 1954, Thai forces occupied the temple. However, Cambodia protested and asked the ICJ to rule that the temple and the surrounding land lay in Cambodian territory.

On June 15, 1962 the ICJ found *"by nine votes to three, ... that the Temple of Preah Vihear is situated in territory under the sovereignty of Cambodia; by nine votes to three, that Thailand is under an obligation to withdraw any military or police forces, or other guards or keepers, stationed by her at the Temple, or in its vicinity on Cambodian territory; by seven votes to five, that Thailand is under an obligation to restore to Cambodia any objects of the kind specified in Cambodia's fifth Submission which may, since the date of the occupation of the Temple by Thailand in 1954, have been removed from the Temple or the Temple area by the Thai authorities."*

---

[80]   ANTHONY AUST, Modern treaty law and practice (2000), p. 302.

2.3.   Compensation

Compensation is the most likely remedy to be sought by a foreign state, especially when its nationals or legal entities have suffered a loss from the host state. If damage has been caused by the illegal act, then the injured state has to be placed in the position it would have been if there has not been a wrongful action or omission, and the legal consequences which flow therefrom. The compensation must encompass not only the losses incurred (*damnum emergens*), but also the gains prevented or lost profits (*lucrum cessans*).[81] However, in practice it is unclear, whether the compensation has to be appropriate or full.[82]

Corfu Channel

International Court of Justice, Reports of judgments, Advisory opinions and orders, The Corfu Channel Case (Merits), Judgment of April 9, 1949

After several encounters from May 1946 to November 1946 in the Corfu Channel between the United Kingdom and the People's Republic of Albania, not only two Royal Navy ships have been damaged, but there has been also a significant loss of life. Thus, the United Kingdom was seeking for reparations in the ICJ. After an initial ruling on jurisdiction in 1948, the ICJ issued separate merits and compensation judgments in 1949.

In this case the ICJ held: *"If, however, the Court is competent to decide what kind of satisfaction is due to Albania ..., it is difficult to see why it should lack competence to decide the amount of compensation which is due to the United Kingdom ... If, however, the Court should limit itself to saying that there is a duty to pay compensation without deciding what amount of compensation is due, the dispute would not be finally decided... For the foregoing*

---

[81]   AUST, op. cit., p. 304 and BORZU SABAHI/NICHOLAS J. BIRCH, Comparative compensation for expropriation, in: International investment law and comparative public law, edited by Stephan W. Schill (2010), p. 768.

[82]   See SORNARAJAH, International law, p. 440; SUSAN BREAU, Questions & answers, international law 2013 and 2014 (2013), p. 156.

> *reasons, the Court has arrived at the conclusion that it has jurisdiction to assess the amount of the compensation...."*
> Eventually, the ICJ awarded the United Kingdom a compensation of £ 843,947.

Generally, there is the idea, which is also expressed in the *"CHORZÓW FACTORY"-case,* that there is a primacy of restitution in kind and therefore it is considered as the main remedy for all breaches of international law.[83] However, restitution in kind is for example not so often awarded in the jurisprudence of ICJ. Thus, compensation has been by far the most used frequently used remedy in international investment disputes.[84]

However, before a lawsuit can be brought to the ICJ, several prerequisites must be met. Among these prerequisites is the so-called principle of *"exhaustion of local effective remedies".* This principle is required by the ICJ because the latter considers it as well-established international customary law.[85]

3.   Legal basis for remedies available to the investors

3.1.   Generally

Traditionally, the principle of state responsibility is only applicable to states. However, as it has been mentioned before, investors from another state can become under certain circumstances the subject to rules of international public law. Thus, the investor can invoke remedies regardless of the fact whether its home state is going to

---

[83]   See ALEXANDER ORAKHELASHVILI, Peremptory norms and reparation for internationally wrongfully acts, in: Baltic Yearbook of international law, Volume 3, edited by Ineta Ziemle, (2003), pp. 35-36. Especially in the context of human rights and humanitarian law, this primacy of restitution becomes more than clear.

[84]   See SERGEY RIPINSKY/KEVIN WILLIAMS, Damages in international investment law (2008), pp. 49 et seq.

[85]   See e.g., Interhandel (Switzerland v. USA), ICJ reports 1959, p. 6 and 27; MALCOLM N. SHAW, International law (2017), p. 620 and PHILIPPE COUVREUR, The international court of justice and the effectiveness of international law (2017), p. 253.

pursue remedies or not. If the acts of a state violate public international law (e.g., breach of a contract between the host state and a foreign investor) and thus that state becomes responsible to an investor, then the injured investor can come forward on the following legal grounds.

3.2. Remedies provided in an international agreement

A BIT between the investors' home state and the state responsible for the injury or even a MIT may provide remedies to an injured investor for the wrongful actions or omissions, and the legal consequences which flow therefrom by the host state.[86]

3.3. Remedies provided in the domestic law of the state responsible for the injury

It is possible that the domestic law of the host state provides remedies to an injured foreign investor.[87] However, pursuing the host state's illegal act by the investor might be pointless as there is a big likelihood that the judges might be unfair, politically biased and/or discriminatory. Thus, the process in the host state might have an unfair outcome.

---

[86] BORZU SABAHI, Compensation and restitution in investor-state arbitration, Principles and practice (2011), p. 11. An *"umbrella clause"* is a treaty provision found in many BITs that requires each contracting state to observe all investment obligations it has assumed with respect to investors from the other contracting state. Such a clause can elevate a contract claim to the level of a treaty claim and thus a violation of an investment contract is deemed to be a violation of the BIT. An example of an umbrella clause is Article X of the Switzerland-Philippines BIT, which provides that *"[e]ach Contracting Party shall observe any obligation it has assumed with regard to specific investments in its territory by investors of the other Contracting Party."* See JARROD WONG, Umbrella clauses in bilateral investment treaties: Of breaches of contract, treaty violations, and the divide between developing and developed countries in foreign investment disputes, 14 Geo. Mason L. Rev. 137 (2006), p. 144.

[87] See JARROD HEPBURN, Domestic law in international investment arbitration (2017), pp. 73 et seq.

3.4.   Remedies provided by investor-state-contracts

It is possible that a state may agree in addition to an existing BIT or MIT to protect the investor's rights on the basis of a contract, in which also possible remedies are awarded to an injured investor for the wrongful actions or omissions, and the legal consequences which flow therefrom by the host state.[88] Such remedies can be found in the contract which generally regulates the specific investment (e.g., an investor acquires shares in a state-owned company and commits to make additional investments by providing a certain amount of capital and to pursue certain business activities). The major difference between these kind of contracts and any other commercial contract between two legal entities is that one of the parties is a state, while the other is a business entity.

---

[88]   José Enrique Alvarez, The public international law regime governing international investment (2011), p. 129.

IV.   Investment insurance

1.   Generally

Investors do not only assess the possible profitability of their endeavors, but they are also concerned with the risks linked to their investments in the host state. Especially, cross border investments are exposed to more risks than domestic investments, as they face not only commercial risks but also political risks. These non-commercial risks include currency issues, restriction of transfer of funds, revenues and/or profits, governmental expropriation or confiscation, civil disturbance, insurrection, civil strife, revolution, war or breach of contract. Particularly with regard to developing countries, these risks affect investments negatively as investors generally want to invest in states that have no or low political risks.[89]

However, the aforementioned non-commercial risks can be mitigated by means of appropriately structured insurances. These insurances are designed to protect an investor against the losses occurring due to specific risks.[90] There are not just private insurance companies, which offer these products, but also international and national financial institutions that provide political risk insurances. These schemes have a positive influence on the investment climate, and many of these insurances have a substantial coverage.[91]

---

[89]   See SALACUSE, The three laws of international investment, p. 258; THOMAS E. KRAYENBUEHL, Cross-border exposures and country risk: Assessment and Monitoring (2001), pp. 42 et seq. and 114-115. and R. BARRY JOHNSTON/İNCI ÖTKER-ROBE, A modernized approach to managing the risks in cross-border capital movements, IMF Policy Working Paper No. 99/6 (1999), p. 8.

[90]   VERNON K. JACOBS/N. RICHARD FOX, Risk management for amateur investors, A guide to higher yields with less risk for nonprofessional investors, plus an analysis of the impact of the new tax law on investors (2003), pp. 10-11.

[91]   See WARRICK SMITH, Covering political and regulatory risks: Issues and options for private infrastructure arrangements, in: Dealing with public risk in private infrastructure, edited by Timothy Irwin/Michael Klein/Guillermo E. Perry/Mateen Thobani (1997), p. 68 and SCOTT L. HOFFMANN, The law and business of

An investor has the following possibilities to insure a cross border investment project.

1.1.   State insurance schemes

Many capital-exporting states operate their own agencies issuing non-commercial risk insurance (e.g., Japan: EID/ MITI, United States: Overseas Private Investment Corporation [OPIC], Germany: TREUARBEIT, United Kingdom: Export Credits Guarantee Department [ECGD], France: Compagnie Française d'Assurance pour le Commerce Extérieur [Coface]). These agencies offer insurance programs, which are in competition with the ones offered by a private insurer.[92] For example, it is somehow more advantageous for an investor from the United States to obtain an insurance from OPIC, because there has to be a BIT between the United States and the host state and after subrogation of the insured claim, the United States will usually not have the same problem with recovery and enforcement as the investor would have.

1.2.   Multilateral international insurance scheme

The Multilateral Investment Guarantee Agency (MIGA) was established in 1988 by an international treaty, operates out of Washington, D.C., United States, and is an enormous organization with 181 member governments (156 developing and 25 industrialized countries). The World Bank supports it. MIGA is the only international insurance scheme.[93]

---

international project finance: a resource for governments, sponsors, lenders, lawyers, and project participants (2001), p. 411.
[92] PRISCILLA A. AHMED/XINGHAI FANG, Project finance in developing countries: IFC's lessons of experience (1999), p. 36.
[93] See https://www.miga.org/history.

1.3. Private insurance schemes

As mentioned, there are also private insurances, which are insuring investment projects in foreign developing countries. However, these insurances are often limited and more expensive than the governmental schemes.[94]

1.4. Combination of these types of insurances

It is possible to combine several of the above-mentioned insurance schemes (e.g., it is possible that a legal entity covers 50% of the non-commercial risks by MIGA and the other 50% by OPIC). Sometimes state insurance schemes work together with MIGA for insuring big projects, and thus are creating a consortium in order to guarantee an insurance coverage for these investments.[95]

2. OPIC (Overseas Private Investment Corporation)

2.1. Generally

As an example of a country insurance scheme, we will have a closer look at the Overseas Private Investment Corporation (OPIC) of the United States. OPIC is an agency of the United States government with the mission to *"foster economic development in new and emerging markets, support U.S. foreign policy and create U.S. jobs by helping U.S. businesses to invest overseas."* The agency does not only provide non-commercial risk insurances, but also provides financing through direct loans and loan guaranties.[96]

OPIC operates on a self-sustaining basis at no net cost to American taxpayers. It generates usual a net income of several hundred million USD per fiscal year. However, the

---

94 AHMED/FANG, op. cit., p. 36.
95 See as an example: Albania, Business and investment opportunities yearbook, Volume 1, Strategic, practical information and opportunities, (2016), p. 220.
96 See https://www.opic.gov/.

insurance and other obligations of OPIC are backed by the full faith and credit of the United States and by OPIC's reserves of several billions USD.

The so-called *"OPIC Charter"* can be found in the Foreign Assistance Act of 1961, sections 231-240b, 22. U.S.C. 2191-2200b.

2.2. Purpose[97]

OPIC mobilizes private capital to help to solve critical development challenges and in doing so, advances United States foreign policy. Because OPIC works with the United States private sector, it encourages American investments abroad, helps United States businesses gain footholds in emerging markets, catalyzing revenues, jobs and growth opportunities and increases the American competitiveness. OPIC achieves its mission by providing investors with financing, guarantees, non-commercial insurance, and support for private equity investment funds.

2.3. Eligible insureds[98]

OPIC requires for the eligible insureds that the investment projects have a meaningful connection to the American private sector. Thus, the OPIC insurance is available to:

- United States citizens;
- corporations, partnerships or other associations created under the laws of the United States, its states or territories, and beneficially owned by American citizens by more than 50 percent;
- foreign corporations that are more than 95 percent owned by investors eligible under the above criteria; and
- other foreign entities that are 100 percent American-owned.

---

[97] https://www.opic.gov/who-we-are/overview.
[98] See the insurance eligibility checklist of OPIC: https://www.opic.gov/doing-business-us/applicant-screener/insurance-eligibility-checklist.

2.4. Eligible host countries

2.4.1. Generally

OPIC is authorized to do business in more than 160 developing and post-conflict countries.[99]

However, there are the following requirements that have to be met by them in order to insure an investment project.

2.4.2. Existence of a BIT

An OPIC is available only to investors undertaking business in a foreign country with which the United States has entered into a BIT.[100] OPIC appears to be the only investment insurance whose relations with host countries are governed by BIT that are specifically negotiated for this purpose. These treaties cover the rights and responsibilities of both home and host governments in relation to OPIC services.

2.4.3. Host government approval of issuance of insurance for each project

All investment projects must receive foreign government approval prior to the issuance of an OPIC insurance. OPIC will provide the investor with guidelines for securing the foreign government approval.[101] Thus, the aforementioned BITs typically have a subrogate provision. If OPIC *"steps into the shoes"* of a legal entity, which has been nationalized, then OPIC has all the rights vis-à-vis that state.

---

[99] See https://www.opic.gov/doing-business-us/OPIC-policies/where-we-operate.

[100] LARRY A. DiMATTEO, International business law and the legal environment: a transactional approach (2017), p. 31. See also SALACUSE, The three laws of international investment, p. 78.

[101] See JOHN W. DUFFY, Andean and Caribbean basin financing directory (1994), p. 7.

2.4.4. Observance of human rights and internationally recognized workers' rights[102]

OPIC ensures through its processes for granting an insurance that projects receive OPIC support, if they:

– respect human rights, including the rights of workers; and
– are undertaken in states that are taking steps to adopt and implement laws that extend internationally recognized worker rights.

The protection of human rights is essential to successful OPIC-supported projects. OPIC's project human rights review is designed to ensure that OPIC-supported projects meet their statutory requirements, as required by the Foreign Assistance Act of 1961. For each project seeking OPIC support, OPIC works in close consultation with the United States Department of State prior to making a final commitment.

2.5. Insurable investments

The *"OPIC Charter"* defines the term *"investment"* as follows: *"... the term "investment" includes any contribution or commitment of funds, commodities, services, patents, processes, or techniques, in the form of (1) a loan or loans to an approved project, (2) the purchase of a share of ownership in any such project, (3) participation in royalties, earnings, or profits of any such project, and (4) the furnishing of commodities or services pursuant to a lease or other contract."* (22 U.S.C. § 2198 (a)).[103] Excluded are projects that negatively affect the American balance of payments and employment as well as casinos, military sales, environmentally harmful activities.

---

[102] https://www.opic.gov/doing-business-us/OPIC-policies/worker-human-rights.

[103] See United States Foreign assistance act of 1961, Sec. 238, p. 140 (https://www.opic.gov/sites/default/files/docs/statute0106.pdf).

2.6.   Insurable risks[104]

2.6.1 Generally

OPIC offers several types of non-commercial risk coverage like currency inconvertibility, expropriation, political violence and more targeted specialty products. It is possible to insure an investment project against all these insurable risks, but this would also mean that the insured party has to pay more premiums. Thus, it is up to each investor to decide what kind of risks he wants to insure.

2.6.2. Currency inconvertibility[105]

Host country currency exchange restrictions can have a disastrous impact on the commercial viability of a project, preventing an investor from converting and transferring profits from his project and return of capital, and ability to meet debt obligations. Coverable host government acts may take many forms, including:

– new, more restrictive foreign exchange regulations;
– failure by an exchange control authority to approve of – or simply to act on – an application for hard currency;
– an unlawful effort by the host government to block funds for repatriation;
– discriminatory host government actions resulting in an inability to convert and transfer local earnings

OPIC inconvertibility coverage can insure conversion and transfer of earnings, returns of capital, principal and interest payments, technical assistance fees, and similar remittances. However, there is no protection against the devaluation of a country's currency. This is considered as a normal commercial risk.

---

[104] https://www.opic.gov/what-we-offer/political-risk-insurance/types-of-coverage.
[105] https://www.opic.gov/what-we-offer/political-risk-insurance/types-of-coverage/currency-inconvertability.

Philip Morris International Finance Corporation

(Dominican Republic: 1989)

Inconvertibility – OPIC Contract of Insurance No. 7137

OPIC issued in 1970 an insurance contract to Philip Morris International Finance Corporation in order to provide an inconvertibility insurance coverage for its investment in E. León Jimenes C. por. A, which was a tobacco corporation in the Dominican Republic. In 1984 the latter applied to the Central Bank of the Dominican Republic for the transfer of the local currency earnings. This request has been denied by the Central Bank based on Monetary Board's resolutions, which regulated all profit remittances to the free exchange market and limited transfers of USD in the amount of USD 200'000 per month.

Subsequently, Philip Morris International Finance Corporation filed a claim with OPIC for inconvertibility. OPIC declared the claim valid because this ruling did not exist at the time Philip Morris executed its contract.

2.6.3. Expropriation and other forms of unlawful government interference[106]

OPIC can protect a foreign investment from expropriatory acts and other forms of unlawful interference by the host government that deprive an investor of his fundamental rights in a project. The traditional expropriation coverage protects against nationalization, confiscation and creeping expropriations, which results in a loss of the total investment. Government interference in a project can take many forms, among them are the following:

- abrogation, repudiation, and/or impairment of contract, including forced renegotiation of contract terms;
- imposing of confiscatory taxes;
- confiscation of funds and/or tangible assets; and
- outright nationalization of a project.

---

[106] https://www.opic.gov/what-we-offer/political-risk-insurance/types-of-coverage/expropriation.

Webster Publishing Co.

Expropriation – OPIC Contract of Insurance No. 894 (Iran: 1966)

The Webster Publishing Co. had an equity investment in Sherkat-Sahami Iran-Webster, which sold books in Iran. Webster Publishing Co. entered into a contract with Iran to supply textbooks to Iranian schools. After the Iranian Revolution in 1976, the new government created its own government printing enterprise. As a result, Iran drove Webster Publishing Co. out of its principal market.

Subsequently, Webster Publishing Co. filed a claim with OPIC for expropriation. OPIC denied Webster Publishing Co.'s claim that this action constituted expropriation. The agency held that the restructuring of the textbook supply system was a legitimate regulatory scheme. OPIC found that this is just a market loss, which is not a covered risk. OPIC made Webster Publishing Co. responsible for regaining the market share lost to the government.

2.6.4. Political violence[107]

In a world of increasing political uncertainty, politically-motivated violence and terrorism can have a crippling impact on the overseas investments of an investor. Thus, OPIC's political violence coverage compensates investors for equity assets (including property) and income losses caused by:

- declared or undeclared war;
- hostile actions by national or international forces;
- revolution, insurrection, and civil strife; and/or
- terrorism and sabotage.

OPIC pays compensation for two types of losses:

- *assets*: damage to covered tangible assets; and
- *business income*: income losses resulting from damage to assets of the foreign enterprise caused by political violence/terrorism.

---

[107] https://www.opic.gov/what-we-offer/political-risk-insurance/types-of-coverage/political-violence.

Investors may purchase one or both coverages. In addition, OPIC can provide coverage for:

- *evacuation expenses*;
- *temporary abandonment*: income losses if the political violence causes the evacuation or forced abandonment of a project; and/or
- *offsite riders*: OPIC can compensate for income losses resulting from damage to specific sites outside the insured facility, such as a critical railway spur, power station, or supplier.

Beckman Instruments, Inc.

War/Revolution/Insurrection – OPIC Contracts of Insurance Nos. 9652 and 9653 (El Salvador: 1982)

Beckman Instruments, Inc. ("*Beckman*") filed a claim to OPIC for losses incurred due to civil strife in El Salvador. The claim arose out of the kidnapping of a citizen of the United States – one of Beckman's engineers – and a Salvadorian manager of the foreign enterprise in 1979 by a terrorist group named "*Partido Revolucionario de Los Trabajadores Centros Americanos*". During this time, El Salvador was suffering from various acts of political violence. However, the kidnappers' demands have been met by Beckman and the hostages were released unharmed. After this event, Beckman decided to stop manufacturing in El Salvador because it was not safe to send safely its personnel to El Salvador in order to train local production workers. Subsequently local workers asked an union for help. The latter tried to convince Beckman to reopen the manufactory. Soon afterwards, these workers and union members seized equipment and were not willing to return it until certain demands were met. Beckman's negotiations with the workers and the union failed. Finally, Beckman filed a claim with OPIC for political violence losses.

OPIC held that these acts were not politically motivated. It was not an act of war, revolution or insurrection. The workers together with the union created a number of violent, demonstrations protesting government policies, but this did not turn the union into an insurrectionist group. Furthermore, the seizure of the equipment was not part of a plan of the political regime in El Salvador.

2.7. Duration

It is possible to link the duration of an insurance with the duration of the investment project. The average duration of an insurance is 20 years, but it also possible to insure longer or shorter periods.[108]

2.8. Premium

Premium rates are set accordingly to a base rate, which is adjustable according to OPIC's assessment of the project risk and which remain applicable for the duration of the investment project. Premium base rates for the coverage of a specific risk range from USD 0.20 to USD 0.80 annually per USD 100.00 of coverage. The base premium for the coverage regarding inconvertibility and expropriation is USD 1.15 per annum for an equity investment in a manufacturing project. The base premium for such a project to cover against loss of both business income and assets due to political violence is an additional USD 1.10 per annum.[109]

3. MIGA (Multilateral Investment Guarantee Agency)

3.1. Generally

MIGA (Multilateral Investment Guarantee Agency) was established in 1988 by an international treaty, is headquartered in Washington D.C., USA, and supported by the World Bank. It was created to promote foreign direct investment into developing countries. The organization was founded with a capital base of USD 1 billion.

Unlike other insurers, MIGA is backed by the World Bank Group and its member countries. According to article 1(b) of the MIGA-Convention MIGA has *"juridical personality"*, and has the right to *"institute legal proceedings"*. MIGA also requires host country government approval for every

---

[108] See SALACUSE, The three laws of international investment, p. 262.
[109] See also DUFFY, op. cit., p. 7.

project. Thus, it tries to work with host governments and to resolve claims before they are filed.

MIGA has paid eight claims since 1988. The first claim was in 2000 for an equity investment in P.T. East Java Power Corporation in Indonesia. The project was one of several power projects suspended by a presidential decree in 1997 in response to the country's economic crisis in the late 1990s. The second claim was for war and civil disturbance relating to a power plant project in Nepal. MIGA paid compensation for the repair of the damages to the gas turbine, and the project continues to be in operation. The third claim was for a project in Argentina at the time of the country's financial crisis. The fourth and fifth claim were paid in fiscal year 2009 and were both related to losses under war and civil disturbance coverage. One was paid for losses incurred in the violence following Kenya's disputed election in 2007 and the other was paid for losses resulting from political violence in Madagascar. In 2011, a small claim for war and civil disturbance was paid from the donor-funded Afghanistan Investment Guarantee Facility. In fiscal 2015 MIGA paid three claims for losses incurred from war and civil disturbance events, in Burkina Faso, Central African Republic, and Mali.

The small number of claims paid by MIGA since 1988 attests to the agency's ability to work with investors and host countries to find amicable resolutions to disputes. MIGA focuses on finding solutions to pre-claim situations before they reach the level of full-fledged claims. MIGA's proactive facilitation efforts have been important in the resolution of more than 90 disputes related to MIGA-guaranteed projects.

3.2.   Purpose

MIGA's stated mission is *"to promote foreign direct investment into developing countries to support economic growth, reduce poverty, and improve people's lives"*. Therefore, it is written in article 2 of the MIGA-Convention that MIGA's principle purpose and objective is to encourage the flow of investment to and among developing countries by means of guarantees. MIGA provides guarantees against non-commercial risks to protect cross border investments in developing member countries. Guarantees protect investors against the risks of transfer restriction, expropriation, war, terrorism and civil disturbance, and breach of contract.

MIGA is based on a multilateral treaty and therefore interesting for countries without national insurance schemes. Furthermore, if for example the United States do not have a BIT with a specific country, then OPIC cannot apply. However, there is still the possibility of obtaining an insurance from MIGA.

3.3.   Eligible insureds[110]

In general, investors who are citizens of, or entities that are incorporated in MIGA member countries – other than the host country, in which the investment is being made – are eligible for MIGA guarantees. However, MIGA can insure an investment made by a national of a host country if the funds to be invested come from outside the country and the application for coverage is made jointly by the investor and the host country.

As nearly every state is member of MIGA, it is possible to get virtually for every country on earth a MIGA-insurance.

3.4.   Eligible host countries

Article 14 MIGA-Convention states that *"[i]nvestments shall be guaranteed … if they are to be made in the territory of a developing member country"*. In order to determine which states are considered to be a developing country, MIGA consults the World Bank's classification list. Additionally, there must be a good investment climate. However, investors can be both developed and developing countries.

---

[110]   See http://www.miga.org/sites/default/files/archive/Documents/ miga_documents/IGGen_old.pdf.

3.5. Insured investments[111]

MIGA insures cross border investments. This includes projects with new investments as well as investments associated with the expansion, modernization, improvement, or enhancement of existing projects, or where the investor demonstrates both the development benefits of, and a long-term commitment to, the project. Acquisitions by new investors, including the privatization of state-owned enterprises, may also be eligible.

Forms of eligible investments include equity interests, shareholder and non-shareholder loans, loan guarantees, as well as certain types of transactions in which the remuneration of the investor largely depends on the revenues or production of the investment project (e.g., technical assistance contracts, management contracts, operating leases, profit sharing contracts, and franchising agreements).

MIGA will not insure unless the investment:

(1) is financially viable,
(2) contributes to the host country,
(3) is consistent with the host country's developing goals,
(4) complies with MIGA's Policy on Social and Environmental Sustainability and Anti-corruption and Fraud Standards, and
(5) has appropriate legal protection for investors in the host country.

Before MIGA insures, it has to evaluate the investment project and thus it will:

(1) do a project assessment,
(2) do a risk assessment,
(3) obtain a host country approval (article 15 MIGA-Convention).

Most sectors are eligible for MIGA guarantees, including (but not limited to) financial, infrastructure, oil and gas, mining, telecommunications, services, agribusiness, and manufacturing. Sectors not eligible for coverage include gambling, tobacco production and processing, highly

---

[111] See http://www.miga.org/sites/default/files/archive/Documents/ miga_documents/IGGen_old.pdf.

speculative investments, defense, illegal drugs, and the production of spirits.

3.6.   Insurable risks[112]

3.6.1. Generally

The insurance guarantees protect investors against the risks of currency inconvertibility and transfer restriction, expropriation, breach of contract (for contracts between the investor/project enterprise and the authorities of the host country), and war, terrorism and civil disturbance. These coverages may be purchased individually or in combination.

3.6.2. Currency inconvertibility and transfer restriction[113]

The insurance for currency inconvertibility and transfer restriction protects against losses arising from an investor's inability to legally convert local currency (capital, interest, principal, profits, royalties, and other remittances) into foreign exchange and/or to transfer local currency or foreign exchange outside the country where such a situation results from a government action or failure to act. Currency depreciation is not covered. In the event of a claim, MIGA pays compensation in the currency specified in the contract of guarantee.

3.6.3. Expropriation[114]

The insurance guarantee for expropriation prevents losses arising from certain government actions that may reduce or eliminate ownership of, control over, or rights to the insured investment. In addition to outright nationalization and confiscation, "*creeping*" expropriation – a series of acts that,

---

[112] See https://www.miga.org/products.
[113] See https://www.miga.org/product/currency-inconvertibility-and-transfer-restriction.
[114] See https://www.miga.org/product/expropriation.

51

over time, have an expropriatory effect – is also covered. Coverage is available on a limited basis for partial expropriation (e.g., confiscation of funds or tangible assets).

In the case of total expropriation of equity investments, compensation to the insured party is based on the net book value of the insured investment. For expropriation of funds, MIGA pays the insured portion of the blocked funds. For loans and loan guaranties, MIGA can insure the outstanding principal and any accrued and unpaid interest. Compensation will be paid upon assignment of the investor's interest in the expropriated investment (e.g., equity shares or interest in a loan agreement) to MIGA.

3.6.4. Breach of contract[115]

The insurance for breach of contract protects against losses arising from the government's breach or repudiation of a contract with the investor. Breach of contract coverage may be extended to the contractual obligations of state-owned enterprises in certain circumstances. In the event of an alleged breach or repudiation, the investor should invoke a dispute resolution mechanism (e.g., an arbitration) set out in the underlying contract. If, after a specified period of time, the investor has been unable to obtain an award due to the government's frustration of its efforts, or has obtained an award but the investor has not received payment under the award, MIGA will pay compensation. If certain conditions are met, MIGA may, at its discretion, make a provisional payment pending the outcome of the dispute. MIGA may also elect to pay compensation without an award, if the investor does not have recourse to a dispute resolution forum or there is unreasonable government interference with the investor's pursuit of legal rights against the host government. The coverages described above may be purchased individually or in combination, but selection of the desired coverages must be made by an investor before MIGA issues its guarantee.

---

[115] See https://www.miga.org/product/breach-contract.

3.6.5. War, terrorism and civil disturbance[116]

The insurance guarantee for war, terrorism and civil disturbance protects against loss from, damage to, or the destruction or disappearance of, tangible assets or total business interruption (the total inability to conduct operations essential to a project's overall financial viability) caused by politically motivated acts of war or civil disturbance in the country, including revolution, insurrection, coups d'état, sabotage, and terrorism. The cover protects against losses directly attributable to the physical damage of assets and total business interruption. For total business interruption, compensation would be based on the net book value of the total insured equity investment or the insured portion of the principal and interest payment in default as a direct result of a covered war and civil disturbance event. For tangible asset losses, MIGA will pay the investor's share of the lesser of the book value of the project assets, their replacement cost, and the cost of repair of the damaged assets.

Temporary business interruption may also be included upon a request from the investor and would cover three sources of interruption: (i) damage of assets, (ii) forced abandonment, and (iii) loss of use. For short-term business interruption, MIGA will pay unavoidable continuing expenses and extraordinary expenses associated with the restart of operations and lost business income or, in the case of loans, missed payments.

This coverage encompasses not only violence in the host country directed against a host country government, but also against foreign governments or foreign investments, including the investor's government or nationality.

---

[116] See https://www.miga.org/product/war-terrorism-and-civil-disturbance.

3.6.6. Non-honoring of financial obligations[117]

The non-honoring of financial obligations coverage provides protection against losses resulting from a failure of a sovereign, sub-sovereign, or state-owned enterprise to make a payment when due under an unconditional financial payment obligation or guarantee related to an eligible investment. It does not require the investor to obtain an arbitral award. This coverage is applicable in situations when a financial payment obligation is unconditional and not subject to defenses. Compensation is based on the insured outstanding principal and any accrued and unpaid interest.

3.7. Duration[118]

MIGA issues guarantees for periods of up to 15 years, and occasionally, 20 years if it is justified by the nature of the project. The minimum length of a guarantee is three years. In guarantees that cover loans, MIGA usually issues coverage to match the length of such loans. MIGA cannot terminate the contract unless the investor defaults on its contractual obligations to MIGA, but the investor may reduce or cancel coverage without penalty on any contract anniversary date starting with the third anniversary.

3.8. Premium[119]

MIGA prices its guarantee premiums based on a calculation of both country and project risk. Fees average is approximately one percent of the insured amount per year, but can be significantly lower or higher.

---

[117] See   https://www.miga.org/product/non-honoring-financial-obligations.
[118] See https://www.miga.org/terms-conditions.
[119] https://www.miga.org/terms-conditions.

4. Private insurance schemes

Since the early 1700s there have been insurers like Lloyd's, who have covered war perils as part of marine risk coverage. However, coverage of land-based war risk had been virtually nonexistent since World War II. But the magnitude of losses that could result from modern warfare made the private insurance market to insure also risks like nationalization, currency inconvertibility, war and political violence, terrorism, and contract cancellation.

Private insurance schemes are attractive for investors who cannot take advantage of MIGA or national schemes like OPIC. Furthermore, the range of possible risks that can be covered is much bigger (e.g., kidnap/ransom/extortion insurances). However, the premiums are substantially higher than the ones of MIGA or OPIC and the duration of the insurance is often not as long as the period of the investment project.

V. Nationalization

1. Generally

Nationalization is the process of taking private property from an owner into public ownership by a state through a wide range of governmental acts.[120] Although nationalization may happen also in developed countries (notably during an economic crisis, as evidenced during the latest crisis in this century), it has nevertheless been more attributed to developing countries. However, nationalization is sometimes indispensable even in developed countries as means to achieve some legitimate public interest (e.g., a state nationalizes private property in order to build a road or other infrastructure projects).

The international law of nationalization has been the subject of various conflicts between developed and developing countries.

The customary international law on nationalization has been developed during the time of confiscations with regard to cross border investment projects.[121] It is noteworthy that following the period of decolonization, revolutions and spreading communism there was an intense period in the 50s and 60s of the last century, when numerous nationalizations and seizures of foreign property happened and the states argued over the lawfulness of these acts and the compensation. Moreover, due to the shortage of oil in the 1970s there have been various oil nationalizations of oil supplies in this decade (e.g., Iraq: 1972; India: 1973 coal industry and oil companies). Furthermore, there were in the

---

[120] Definition found on: https://www.merriam-webster.com/dictionary/nationalization. The opposite of nationalization is usually privatization or de-nationalization.

[121] See also ANDREW NEWCOMBE/LLUÍS PARADELL, Law and practice of investment treaties, standards of treatment (2009), p. 322 and American International Group, Inc./American Life Insurance Company and Islamic Republic of Iran/Central Insurance of Iran (Bimeh Markazi Iran), Case No. 2, Award No. 93-2-3.

last years some cases of expropriations in relation with foreign investments in the energy sector.[122]

Types of nationalizations in the broader sense in the field of cross border investment projects[123]

(i)   Expropriation

Expropriation is when a state takes over a foreign investment in a country by the state or a state-mandated third party.

(ii)   Nationalization

Nationalization is when a state takes over a whole sector of economy with its foreign investments in a country by the state or a state-mandated third party.

(iii)   Confiscation

Confiscation is an unlawful takeover of a foreign investment by the state or a state-mandated third party.

Furthermore, it is possible to subdivide expropriation, nationalization and confiscation into:

(i)   Direct expropriation/nationalization/confiscation

A direct expropriation/nationalization happens if a state passes or applies a specific legislation to takeover another's property.

(ii)   Indirect expropriation/nationalization/confiscation

An indirect expropriation/nationalization/confiscation happens when the foreign investor is losing the control or economic value of his investment project through the

---

[122] E.g., nationalization of banks in Greece, Iceland, the Netherlands, Portugal, but there are also examples of nationalization of other industries, notably those of general economic interest (e.g. recently, in Japan and United Kingdom). See also BREAU, op. cit., pp. 155 et seq. and JOHN WILLMAN, Nationalisation: a blast from the past, in: Financial Times (January 18, 2018).

[123] See ROGER E. MEINERS/AL. H. RINGLEB/FRANCES L. EDWARDS, The legal environment of business (2018), p. 549 and NEWCOMBE/PARADELL, op. cit., pp. 324 et seq.

interference by the host state, even when the legal title of the investment is not affected.

(iii)   Creeping expropriation/nationalization/confiscation

Creeping   expropriation/nationalization/confiscation happens incrementally or step by step through a series of separate governmental measures or acts, none of which might   qualify   as   an   expropriation/ nationalization/confiscation by itself, but altogether they have the effect to destroy the value of the investment and lead also to a de facto dispossession.

2.   Legality of nationalization

2.1.   General rule

Most of the tribunals, state practice and international instruments are of the opinion that a state can nationalize private property or even a sector whenever it wants. The base of this rule is the territorial sovereignty of a state and the legality of the act is founded on the willingness to pay a compensation.

A state may nationalize the property of foreign investors within its borders in a lawful way, if

(1) the nationalization is based on a public interest/purpose;
(2) it has been taken following proper law proceedings;
(3) it is non-discriminatory; and
(4) a compensation will be paid.

2.1.1.   Case law

Ethyl Corporation v. the Government of Canada

Award on jurisdiction in the NAFTA/UNCITRAL case between Ethyl Corporation and the Government of Canada, June 24, 1998

In April 1997 the Government of Canada passed a law restricting the import and interprovincial transport of the

58

neuro-toxic MMT, a gasoline additive that contains the heavy metal manganese.

On April 15, 1997, Ethyl Corporation, an American legal entity with a Canadian subsidiary, invoked the *"expropriation-clause"* (article 1110) of the investment chapter of NAFTA to sue the Government of Canada for CAD 350 million for damages and lost income, because the law was a measure tantamount to an expropriation.

On July 20, 1998, the Government of Canada decided to settle the dispute. It issued a statement that the manganese-based additive is neither a health nor an environmental risk and paid a compensation of CAD 19.5 million to the Ethyl Corporation.

Methanex Corporation v. United States of America

Decision on amici curiae: Methanex Corporation v United States, Ad hoc—UNCITRAL Arbitration Rules; IIC 165 (2001), January 15, 2001

Partial award: Methanex Corporation v. United States, Ad hoc—UNCITRAL Arbitration Rules; IIC 166 (2002), August 7, 2002

Methanex, a Canadian company, is a major producer of methanol, a key component in MTBE (methyl tertiary butyl ether), which is used to increase the oxygen content and can act as an octane enhancer for unleaded gasoline.

The Californian government enacted a law banning the use of MTBE in reformulated gasoline in California, because it was of the opinion that the additive is contaminating drinking water supplies, and is therefore posing a significant risk to human health, safety, and the environment.

In response, Methanex and its American subsidiaries launched an international arbitration against the United States. The company argued that the law is ineffective and non-enforcement of domestic environmental laws is responsible for the presence of MTBE in California water supplies. Furthermore, it invoked the *"expropriation-clause"* (article 1110) of the investment chapter of NAFTA and argued that the planned ban is tantamount to an expropriation of the company's investment as it was not anymore allowed to sell these products. Thus, the legal entity was seeking financial compensation from the United States in the amount of over USD 900 million.

On August 9, 2005, the tribunal released the final award, dismissing all of the claims. The Tribunal ordered Methanex to pay the United States' legal fees and arbitral expenses in the amount of approximately USD 4 million.

The tribunal undertook an extensive review of the process by which California enacted its ban and held in a final award that (Final Award, Part IV, Chapter D, para 7 and 15): *"In the Tribunal's view, Methanex is correct that an intentionally discriminatory regulation against a foreign investor fulfils a key requirement for establishing expropriation. But as a matter of general international law, a non-discriminatory regulation for a public purpose, which is enacted in accordance with due process and, which affects, inter alias, a foreign investor or investment is not deemed expropriatory and compensable unless specific commitments had been given by the regulating government to the then putative foreign investor contemplating investment that the government would refrain from such regulation ... For reasons elaborated here and earlier in this Award, the Tribunal concludes that the California ban was made for a public purpose, was non-discriminatory and was accomplished with due process. Hence, Methanex's central claim under Article 1110(1) of expropriation under one of the three forms of action in that provision fails. From the standpoint of international law, the California ban was a lawful regulation and not an expropriation."*

Ronald S. Lauder v. the Czech Republic

Final award UNCITRAL arbitration, September 3, 2001

In the final award it was held that: *"The Bilateral Investment Treaties generally do not define the term of expropriation and nationalization, or any of the other terms denoting similar measures of forced dispossession ("dispossession", "taking", "deprivation", or "privation"). Furthermore, the practice shows that although the various terms may be used either alone or in combination, most often no distinctions have been attempted between the general concept of dispossession and the specific forms thereof. In general, expropriation means the coercive appropriation by the state of private property, usually by means of individual administrative measures. Nationalization involves large-scale takings on the basis of an executive or legislative act for the purpose of transferring property or interests into the public domain. The concept of indirect (or "de facto", or "creeping") expropriation is not clearly defined. Indirect expropriation or nationalization is a measure that does not involve an overt taking, but that effectively neutralizes the enjoyment of the property. It is generally accepted that a wide variety of measures are susceptible to lead to indirect expropriation, and each case is therefore to be decided on the basis of its attending circumstances (Rudolf Dolzer & Margrete Stevens, Bilateral Investment Treaties, p. 98-100 (1995); Georgio Sacerdoti, Bilateral Treaties and Multilateral Instruments on Investment Protection, 379-382 (1997)). The European Court of Human Rights in Mellacher and Others v. Austria (1989 Eur.Ct.H.R. (ser. A, No. 169)), held that a "formal" expropriation is a measure aimed at a "transfer of property", while a "de facto" expropriation occurs when a state deprives the owner of his "right to use, let or sell (his) property".*

2.1.2. State practice

Hull principle[124]

United States State Department Letter to the Mexican Government (1938)

In 1938 the United States Secretary of State Cordell Hull held in a letter to the Mexican government regarding the nationalization of certain agrarian and oil properties, that expropriation of foreign owned property is legitimate but it must be accompanied by *"prompt, adequate, and effective compensation"*. According to this view, the nationalizing

---

[124] FRANK G. DAWSON/BURNS H. WESTON, "Prompt, adequate and effective": a universal standard of compensation?, in: 30 Fordham L. Rev. (1962), pp. 733-734; DAVID COLLINS, An introduction of international investment law (2017), p. 188 and SORNARAJAH, International law, p. 210.

state is obligated under international law to pay the deprived party the full value of the property taken.

2.1.3. International instruments

1962 General Assembly Resolution 1803 (XVII): The declaration on permanent sovereignty over natural resources

In 1962, the United Nations General Assembly adopted Resolution 1803, *"Permanent Sovereignty over National Resources"*, which states in article 4 that in the event of nationalization, the owner *"shall be paid appropriate compensation in accordance with international law."*

Energy Charter Treaty

The Energy Charter Treaty (ECT) is an international agreement, which establishes a multilateral framework for cross border co-operations in the energy industry. The treaty covers all aspects of commercial energy activities including trade, transit, investments and energy efficiency. The treaty is legally binding and includes dispute resolution procedures.

Article 13 of the ECT provides a guarantee that both direct and indirect forms of expropriation of an investment shall only take place against prompt effective and adequate compensation, by following due process and on a non-discriminatory basis. This is similar to the guarantee found in most of the BITs, including those signed by ECT member countries.

Article 13(1) states the following: *"Investments of Investors of a Contracting Party in the Area of any other Contracting Party shall not be nationalized, expropriated or subjected to a measure or measures having effect equivalent to nationalization or expropriation (hereinafter referred to as "Expropriation") except where such Expropriation is:*

(a) for a purpose which is in the public interest;
(b) not discriminatory;
(c) carried out under due process of law; and

(d) accompanied by the payment of prompt, adequate and effective compensation."

2.2. Public interest/purpose of the nationalization

Different countries have different views about what is a public interest or public purpose, which justifies a nationalization. *"Public Purpose"* has been defined as *"reasons of public utility, judicial liquidation and similar measures"* (CHORZÓW FACTORY). Thus, challenging a nationalization based on a claim that was not in the *"public interest"* would possibly be effective in the case of a dictator seizing property clearly for his personal use.[125] In any event, public purpose or public interest is a legal standard which is generally not defined by legislation *in abstracto*, but it is rather imperative to take into account all the circumstances of the individual case.

Siderman de Blake v. Republic of Argentina

(Siderman de Blake v. Republic of Argentina, 965 F.2d. 699 [9th Cir.] 1992)

The night before the overthrow of the Argentine government by the military in 1976, an Argentine citizen was tortured, and he, his wife, and his son were expelled from Argentina. In addition, Argentina expropriated an Argentine corporation owned by the family through a sham *"judicial intervention"* in 1977. Included among the property of this corporation was the hotel *"Gran Corona"*, in Tucumán, Argentina.

The Sidermans' brought suit it the United States District Court, but the court dismissed the expropriation claims. The Sidermans' appealed to the Ninth Circuit Court of Appeals, which held that the actions of the Argentine government fell within the *"commercial activities"* exception of the US Foreign Sovereign Immunities Act (FISA), and remanded the case to the district court. In particular, the court held that the Sidermans' claim was *"based upon a commercial activity carried on in the United States by the foreign state."*

---

125 See NEWCOMBE/PARADELL, op. cit., p. 371.

First, Argentina's continuous management and operation of the hotel, and receipt of profits from the hotel, were commercial activities in which a private party might engage. Second, these activities were being carried on in the United States, due to the advertising of the hotel in the United States and the solicitation of American guests through the national airline of Argentina, which was its agent. The hotel also accepted American credit cards.

Thus, the Argentine government expropriated a hotel in which a citizen of the United States of America held an interest. Furthermore, the court held that actions by the Argentinian government violated international law:

(i)   *Public Purpose of Expropriation*: The hotel was taken for the profit of the government, and not for any public purpose.

(ii)   *Expropriation was discriminatory*: Since it was based on the fact that the Sidermans' were Jews; Christians were not expropriated.

(iii)   *Compensation*: No compensation for the expropriated hotel was paid.

Based on this, the court held that the expropriation was illegal under international law, and the sovereign immunity defense was not effective.

2.3.   Property has been taken following proper law proceedings

The domestic law of the host state has to be enacted following the proper law proceedings, and to precise the process for carrying out a nationalization of the investor's properties. There has to be *"an actual and substantive legal procedure for a foreign investor to raise its claims against the depriving actions already taken or about to be taken against it. Some basic legal mechanisms, such as reasonable advance notice, a fair hearing and an unbiased and impartial adjudicator to assess the actions in dispute, are expected to be readily available and accessible to the investor to make such legal procedure meaningful."*[126]

Proper law proceedings comprise any issue in connection with the process which determines an objective evaluation of the process, such as what should be taken into account, limitations to discretionary powers, which state body of law has to make a decision, time limit for the decision, appropriate recourse before the court of law etc. Since courts are often also involved in the process (and preferably a court makes the decision and not a government's ministry, agency or other office of the executive branch), the appropriateness of the whole process is intrinsically linked with the general position of the judiciary and its independence, fairness, objectivity and impartiality.

2.4. Non-discrimination

An expropriation must also be *"non-discriminatory"* to be considered *"legal"* under international law.

Oscar Chinn

PCIJ Series A/B No. 63 (1934)

The Permanent Court of International Justice defined discrimination as follows (para. 93): *"The form of discrimination which is forbidden is therefore discrimination based upon nationality and involving differential treatment by reason of their nationality as between persons belonging to different national groups."*

A discriminatory taking is a taking that unreasonably singles out a particular person or group of people, i.e., when a specific nationality is targeted.[127] Thus, in 1959 the

---

[126] See ADC Affiliate Limited and ADC & ADMC Management Limited v. Republic of Hungary, ICSID Case No. ARB/03/16, Serial No. 120, para. 434 et seq.; C. L. LIM/JEAN HO/MARTINS PAPARINSKIS, International investment law and arbitration, (2018), pp. 343-344 and KRISTA NADAKAVUKAREN SCHEFER, International investment law, text, cases and materials (2016), pp. 204-205.

[127] See also the aforementioned case SIDERMAN DE BLAKE V. REPUBLIC OF ARGENTINA.

Indonesian nationalizations of Dutch property were clearly violations of the international law.[128] Broadly speaking, most often discrimination in nationalization cases is based on nationality. However, discrimination on any ground (gender, religion, sexual orientation, age, place of residence, financial census etc.) should be discouraged and not be permitted.

2.5. Compensation

2.5.1 Generally

It is the generally accepted view in the field of public international law, that a nationalization requires the payment of a compensation. Already in older cases the tribunals stated this rule (see for example CHORZÓW FACTORY). Also, in modern tribunal decisions like in the ETHYL CORPORATION V. THE GOVERNMENT OF CANADA or newer ICSID-decisions it is held that a compensation must be paid.

However, if the nationalization is considered illegal, then the host state has usually to restitute in kind and if this is not possible, it has very often to pay damages, which go beyond a compensation as they include a *"punishment"*.

Chorzów Factory

Factory at Chorzow (Germ. v. Pol.), Series A.-No. 17, September 13, 1928, Collection of Judgments, No. 13, Case concerning the factory at Chorzów, para. 125:

"The essential principle contained in the actual notion of an illegal act – a principle which seems to be established by international practice and in particular by the decisions of arbitral tribunals – is that reparation must, as far as possible, wipe-out all the consequences of the illegal act and re-establish the situation which would, in. all probability, have existed if that act had not been committed. Restitution in kind, or, if this is not possible, payment of a sum corresponding to the value which a restitution in kind would bear; the award, if need be, of damages for loss

---

[128] See also DAMOS DUMOI AGUSMAN, Treaties under Indonesian law: A comparative study (2014), p. 8 and LOWENFELD, op. cit., p. 522.

sustained which would not be covered by restitution in kind or payment in place of it-such are the principles which should serve to determine the amount of compensation due for an act contrary to international law."

2.5.2. Full compensation v. appropriate compensation

Although there is the common opinion that in the event of a nationalization a compensation has to be paid, there are different views whether the compensation has to be full or appropriate.

(i)   Full compensation

In order to indemnify a foreign investor fully, the compensation has to encompass the value of structures, machines, business, goodwill and future profits. Even though this standard of compensation is supported by the majority of capital-exporting states, customary practice is in this regard not uniform. Most states have subscribed to the standard of full compensation in BITs, though in some MITs the same states have promoted different standards.[129] As mentioned before, UNITED STATES SECRETARY OF STATE CORDELL HULL held in his letter to the Mexican Government that the consideration has to be *"full (adequate), prompt, effective."* This state practice has for example also been restated in article 13(1) ECT and means the following.

(i.1)   Full/Adequate

The criteria *"adequate"* refers to the question of the amount. Eventually, a foreign investor has to be in the same position as if his property has not been nationalized. This means that

---

[129] See SORNARAJAH, International law, p. 417 and 437 and GUIGUO WANG, International investment law: a Chinese perspective (2015), p. 450.

he has to receive the market value of its investment project (assets etc.) including future profits.[130]

(i.2) Prompt

The payment of the compensation has to be paid quickly after the nationalization. There should not be any unreasonable delay (e.g., the compensation will be paid from the future profits of the nationalized legal entity).[131]

(i.3) Effective

The currency, in which the compensation will be paid, should be freely convertible; a payment in local currency is not considered as effective.[132]

(ii) Appropriate compensation

However, there is also the view that the amount of the compensation has to be decided on a case-by-case basis and therefore the compensation has to be *"appropriate"* (e.g., article 4 of the General Assembly Resolution 1803 [XVII]: The declaration on permanent sovereignty over natural resources).[133] This means in order to determine the compensation a tribunal has to look at the excessive profits, investments, ability of host state to pay the indemnification, the caused environmental damage etc. Furthermore, a state

---

[130] See SERGEY RIPINSKY/KEVIN WILLIAMS, Damages in international investment law (2008), p. 71 and SANGWANI PATRICK NG'AMBI, Resource nationalism in international investment law (2016), pp. 78-79. Market value is the price an asset will get in the market place.

[131] See DAVID COLLINS, An introduction to international investment law (2017), p. 188 and JUNJI NAKAGAWA, Nationalization, natural resources and international investment law, contractual relationship as a dynamic bargaining process (2018), p. 128.

[132] See ALAN W. FORD, The Anglo-Iranian oil dispute of 1951-1952: a study of the role of law in the relations of states (1954), p. 324 and E. I. NWOGUGU, The legal problems of foreign investment in developing countries (1965), p. 56.

[133] See NG'AMBI, op. cit., pp. 80-81.

just wants to pay the compensation based on the book value.[134]

This standard represents more the position of developing countries as the *"appropriate compensation"*-standard allows them to pay less than full compensation following a nationalization. This idea was also supported by the so-called *"Calvo Doctrine"*, which requires that the compensation should be determined by local law, because it is a question of sovereignty.[135]

(iii)   Application by tribunals and courts

National courts as well as tribunals applied public international law on the question of the legality of a nationalization and compensation. In these judicial precedents, which are according to article 38 of the ICJ-Statute a source of international law, it has been held that nationalizations are legal as long as all the aforementioned conditions are respected. However, with regard to the standard of the compensation, it is not clear to which of the two approaches the judges tend to follow.

There are various tribunal decisions (e.g., CHORZÓW FACTORY or BARCELONA TRACTION), which favor the *"full compensation-standard"*. However, there have been contrary views like in the below mentioned AMINOIL-CASE, where it was considered on the question of compensation, that it is possible to advocate an *"appropriate compensation"*.

---

[134] See ADAMU KYUKA USMAN, Theory and practice of international economic law (2017), p. 216. The net book value is the value of an asset in the books of a legal entity.

[135] OECD, International investment law, a changing landscape, a companion volume to international investment perspectives (2005), p. 44 and DAVID COLLINS, The BRIC states and outward foreign direct investment (2013), p. 205.

Aminoil

Award in the matter of an arbitration between Kuwait and the American Independent Oil Company (AMINOIL)

Vol. 21, No. 5 (September 1982), pp. 976-1053

In 1948 a so-called *"colonial-concession"* for 60 years was given by the United Kingdom to the American Independent Oil Company (AMINOIL) in order to exploit oil in Kuwait. Before the 60 years period was over, the government of Kuwait revoked the agreement in passing a law (decree) and took over the operation. AMINOIL alleged that this was illegal, and wanted to characterize this as an international dispute in order to get out of domestic courts. However, the validity of this decree had to be argued, because AMINOIL alleged that the nationalization was discriminatory.

1) Discriminatory nationalization

AMINOIL said that they were discriminated because the nationalization just touched an American company; nothing has been done to the Arabian Oil Company, which was in the similar situation. Therefore, not the totality of the sector was affected, and thus it is not a nationalization. The Court held that the operations of the aforementioned companies were under objective criteria different. There have been adequate reasons for not nationalizing the legal entity, because it had a much more complex production (high-cost off-shore production, which required a high degree of expertise, and therefore it was not that easy to take-over), and also the concession was different. Furthermore, there was nothing in the law, which showed that the government of Kuwait was only after American companies. Kuwait had nationalized over 90 % of the petroleum production in its territory.

2) Infringement of stabilization clauses

In the Concession Agreement of 1948 were the following provisions: Article 1: *"The period of this Agreement shall be sixty (60) years from the date of signature."*; Article 17: *"The Sheikh shall not by general or by administrative measures or by any other act whatever annul this Agreement ... No alteration shall be made in the terms of this Agreement by either the Sheikh or the Company except in the event of the Sheikh and the Company jointly agreeing that it is desirable in the interest of both parties to make certain alterations, deletions or additions to this agreement.*" In 1961 a new Article 11 was provided for the Concession Agreement of 1948: "*... this Agreement shall not be terminated before the expiration of the period specified in Article 1 ...*".

With regard to these provisions AMINOIL maintained the view that these clauses constituted so-called "*stabilization-clauses*" of the contract, and a straightforward and direct reading of them lead to the conclusion that they prohibit any nationalization. The Government of Kuwait argued that, on the contrary, these clauses did not prevent a nationalization, because:

1. the provisions of the Kuwait Constitution prevent the state from granting stabilization guarantees by contract; and

2. permanent sovereignty over natural resources has become an imperative rule of *jus cogens* prohibiting states from affording, by contract or by treaty, guarantees of any kind against the exercise of the public authority in regard to all matters relating to natural riches.

The Court held that it did not appear from the constitutional provisions that they prevented in any way the state from granting stabilization guarantees by contract. Furthermore, domestic law cannot be used as e defense for violating international law, especially if the state has deliberately agreed to enter into a contract/treaty. And with regard to the last argument that even if United Nations General Assembly Resolution 1803 (XVII) adopted in 1962, is to be regarded as reflecting the state of international law, such is not the case with subsequent resolutions which have not the same degree of authority. Even if some of their provisions can be regarded as codifying rules that reflect international practice, it would not be possible from this to deduce the existence of a rule of international law prohibiting a state from undertaking not to proceed to nationalization during a limited period of time. No rule from public international law prevents a state from nationalizing. Moreover, the "*stabilization*" clauses do not prevent a state from nationalizations. However, clauses like the ones *in casu* create legitimate expectations of AMINOIL that they can invest and subsequently make business in Kuwait for a period of 60 years.

3) Standard of compensation

The tribunal rejected that the compensation has to be made on the book value of the nationalized foreign investment, because in this situation it is not appropriate. It took a case by case approach in order to see what is appropriate and held the following: *"The Tribunal considers that the determination of the amount of an award of "appropriate" compensation is better carried out by means of an enquiry into all the circumstances relevant to the particular concrete case..."* Furthermore, the *legitimate expectation* has to be compensated. AMINOIL had because of the *"stabilization"*-clause a legitimate expectation in a *"reasonable rate of return"*. The tribunal looked at the case, the history, the behavior of AMINOIL and referred to the *"appropriate compensation"* as the applicable standard as it cited Article 4 of United Nations General Assembly Resolution 1803 (XVII) of December 14 1962 instead of a full compensation.

VI. Settlement of investment disputes and arbitration

1. Introduction

1.1. Generally

With the growth of international business and cross border transactions, international investment disputes have become also more common. Parties of an international investment dispute can resolve their disputes either by courts or by alternative dispute resolution.

1.2. Domestic courts

If an investor is suing in his home country the host state, then it is likely that the court will take into consideration issues like the sovereign immunity of the host state or the so-called "*act of state doctrine*".

1.3. Foreign courts

If a foreign investor is suing the host state in one of its courts, then there is a probability that the decision will be biased and thus not fair or independent. Furthermore, there is a likelihood that the court of the host state will hold that for example the nationalization was legal and maybe even that the investor is not entitled for receiving a compensation and/or damages.[136]

---

[136] CHRISTOPHER F. DUGAN/DON WALLACE, JR./NOAH D. RUBINS/ BORZU SABAHI, Investor-state arbitration (2013), pp. 15 et seq., which state that the efficiency of a foreign court is a concern of many foreign investors, because developing countries often lack responsive, robust legal systems capable of effectively and quickly adjudicating complex claims.

1.4.   International Court of Justice

According to Article 54 of the ICJ-Statutes, only states can bring claims to the ICJ and thus for an investor the possibilities of an access to this court are limited. An investor would seek the protection of its home state when it unsuccessfully seeks appropriate redress before host state domestic courts or administrative organs following the violations of its rights. In turn, the home state would espouse the investors' claim and resort to diplomatic protection.[137] For example, if a Swiss investor is able to convince the Swiss government to take up his case, then the government becomes literally the *"owner"* of the claim and it controls the case. Thus, the investor loses the control of it. Furthermore, there is also the risk that the government might not sue, because it prefers to pursue other means against the other state (e.g., sanctions, cutting off aid, diplomatic discussions etc.).

Mavrommatis Palestine Concessions

Greece v. UK

1924 P.C.I.J. (ser. B) No. 3 (Aug. 30)

In this decision the ICJ held the following: *"It is true that the dispute was at first between a private person and a State ... Subsequently, the Greek Government took up the case. The dispute then entered upon a new phase; it entered the domain of international law, and became a dispute between two states... It is an elementary principle of international law that a State is entitled to protect its subjects, when injured by acts contrary to international law committed by another state, from whom they have been unable to obtain satisfaction through the ordinary channels. By taking up the*

---

[137] See FAROUK EL-HOSSENY, Civil society in investment treaty arbitration, status and prospects (2018), p. 81. Furthermore, the requirements for starting an ICJ-procedure are the following: (i) exhaustion of local remedies; (ii) there must be a meaningful connection between the investor and the state (see case NOTTEBOHM or BARCELONA TRACTION), (iii) there must be a consent of the state, which has to take up the case for the investor (i.e., one of its individual/legal entity), and (iv) the state being sued has to give his consent.

case of one of its subjects and by resorting to diplomatic action or international judicial proceedings on his behalf, a state is in reality asserting its own rights - its right to ensure, in the person of its subjects, respect for the rules of international law. The question, therefore, whether the present dispute originates in an injury to a private interest, which in point of fact is the case in many international disputes, is irrelevant from this standpoint. Once a State has taken up a case on behalf of one of its subjects before an international tribunal, in the eyes of the latter the state is sole claimant."

1.5.   Alternative dispute resolution

A common division of various alternative dispute resolution mechanisms is the following: negotiation, mediation, and arbitration.[138] Especially the latter is of interest with regard to foreign investments in developing countries.[139]

2.   Arbitration

International commercial arbitration has become a frequently-used and preferred mechanism to settle commercial disputes. The parties to a dispute refer to arbitration by an arbitral tribunal, which consists of one or more arbitrators, and they agree to be bound by the arbitration decision (i.e., arbitral award), which is legally binding on both sides and enforceable in domestic courts.[140]

---

[138] Some jurisdictions, nevertheless, provide either generally or only for some specific kind of disputes, also for some hybrid alternative dispute resolution types (e.g., facilitation, mini-trial, neutral third-party evaluation, expert determination etc.).

[139] See LEON E. TRAKMAN, Australia's rejection of investor-state arbitration: A sign of global change, in: Regionalism in international investment law, edited by Leon E. Trakman/Nicola W. Ranieri (2013), pp. 345 et seq., who states that Australia is probably the first developed state to openly indicate that it will no longer agree to arbitration within its BITs or regional MITs.

[140] See UCHEORA ONWUAMAEGBU, International dispute settlement mechanisms – Choosing between institutionally supported and ad

This kind of 'general' commercial arbitration is different from investment arbitration. Although both are arbitrations and have some similarities (e.g., both are alternative dispute resolution methods, disputes are decided by a neutral panel of arbitrators/or one arbitrator, the awards should be readily enforceable, the procedure is basically the same), there are major differences between them. Some of these differences may be summarized as follows:

– parties in a commercial arbitration are two private individuals or legal entities, while in an investment arbitration one party is always a state (or e.g., a state agency or other state entity or body) and the other is a foreign investor;

– while a commercial arbitration is based on a arbitration clause in the commercial contract of the parties, the basis of an investment arbitration is most often a BIT (which is between two states) or a MIT (e.g., Energy Charter Treaty) foreseeing submission of disputes between the host state and a foreign investor to an arbitration;

– in commercial arbitration, the single relevant international law legislation is the New York Convention on Recognition and Enforcement of Foreign Arbitral Awards (1958) and, on the other hand, for investment arbitrations relevant are various BITs, MITs and multilateral treaties such as ICSID Convention, Energy Charter Treaty;

– for commercial arbitration, some national law is most often applicable either expressly by the will of the contracting parties (choice of law clauses) or if the contract is silent on the applicable substantive law, then the rules of private international law (with the intervention of arbitrators) would lead to the application of some national law. In investment arbitrations, generally the same rules apply but the choice of law clause and reference to the domestic law of the host state would be interpreted as including also all changes of that law occurring after the investment of the foreign investor took place;

hoc; and between institutions, in: Arbitration under international investment agreements, a guide to the key issues, edited by Katia Yannaca-Small (2010), p. 64.

- in investment arbitrations issues raised are often politically sensitive, while that is usually not the case in commercial arbitrations;
- while commercial arbitrations are commonly covered by confidentiality, not public and the awards are not published, investment arbitrations are, due to involvement of states and possible consequences on the state budget always under more scrutiny of the public and media in the host state and, consequently, at least the essential contents of the arbitral awards are made public;
- investment arbitrations are subject to a specialized institution (e.g., ICSID), even though they may be submitted to a non-governmental arbitration institution or an ad hoc arbitration (as provided by the legal document which is the basis for the arbitration), which is always the case with commercial arbitration.

3. Categories of arbitration

3.1. Generally

For example, there are the following categories of arbitration on which the parties of an international investment project can agree or to which states already agreed in BITs or MITs.[141]

3.2. Institutional arbitration

Institutions like the International Chamber of Commerce (ICC), London Court of Arbitration (LCIA), Arbitration Institute of the Stockholm Chamber of Commerce (SCC) etc. developed the rules in statutes for how arbitration has to be conducted (arbitration rules), and they provide facilities and administer support. The idea is to supply a complete framework for arbitration. Many of these institutional

---

[141] See TAIDA BEGIC, Applicable law in international investment disputes (2005), p. 7 and MICHAEL MCILWRATH/JOHN SAVAGE, International arbitration and mediation: A practical guide (2010), pp. 39 et seq. with a more comprehensive overview of possible arbitral institutions which can be chosen.

frameworks set out default provisions, which are applicable when the parties do not specify these points in the arbitration agreement or contract (e.g., the number of arbitrators).[142] Further, this kind of arbitration is primarily just for private parties, because it is not possible to force states to accept this kind of jurisdiction, even though it is possible that investment disputes could be subject to an arbitration of a non-governmental arbitration institution. Although institutional arbitration requires payment of a fee to the administering institution, the functions performed by the institution can be critical in ensuring that the arbitration proceeds to a final award with a minimum of disruption and without the need for recourse to local courts.[143]

3.3.   Ad hoc arbitration

It is also possible to start an arbitration proceeding ad hoc and thus outside of an institutional framework. In ad hoc cases, the arbitration will be administered by the arbitrators themselves. However, should problems arise in setting the arbitration in motion or in constituting the arbitral tribunal, the parties may have to require the assistance of a state court, or that of an independent appointing authority such as ICC.[144] Furthermore, UNCITRAL Arbitration Rules can be used by an ad hoc arbitration tribunal, because they are not tied to any institution.[145]

3.4.   Treaty-based arbitration institution

For example, in 1965 the World Bank Executive Directors responded to a void in the resolution of international disputes between states and foreign investors by approving the *"Convention on the Settlement of Investment Disputes between States and Nationals of Other States"* (so-called *"ICSID-Convention"*). This convention established the International Centre for Settlement of Investment Disputes

---

[142] MCILWRATH/SAVAGE, op. cit., pp. 39 et seq.
[143] See also https://iccwbo.org/dispute-resolution-services/.
[144] MICHAEL MCILWRATH/JOHN SAVAGE, op. cit., pp. 62 et seq.
[145] BEGIC, op. cit., p. 7.

(ICSID), which offers states and foreign nationals a comprehensive voluntary system of arbitration or conciliation for the resolution of investment disputes.[146] ICSID gives procedural and institutional support and administers investment disputes between states and foreign investors. Currently there are 154 contracting states to the ICSID-Convention.

4. Arbitration procedure

4.1. Arbitration clause

4.1.1. Generally

In commercial contracts, parties, who are entering into a cross border agreement, do usually not think that their endeavor might create a dispute. However, while the parties are drafting the terms of the agreement, it would be prudent for the parties to opt already at this stage in their agreement for arbitration as a form of dispute settlement. Thus, it is advisable to add an arbitration clause in a carefully drafted, written agreement. This applies also to investment contracts.

Furthermore, the parties should also stipulate in the arbitration clause itself:[147]

- the law governing the contract (*"choice-of-law-clause"*),
- the number of arbitrators (e.g., three arbitrators),
- the place of arbitration (it might be important to choose the place of arbitration also with regard to the future enforcement of the award),
- institutional or ad hoc arbitration (if the parties opt for institutional arbitration, then they need to choose also the institution), and
- the language of the arbitration.

Such arbitration clauses are commonly part of the commercial contract between the contracting parties or, in case of lack of an arbitration clause in the contract, parties

---

[146] See ONWUAMAEGBU, op. cit., pp. 65-66.
[147] See PAUL D. FRIEDLAND, Arbitration clauses for international contracts (2007), pp. 61 et seq. with his list of necessary, recommended, and optional elements.

may agree on arbitration once the dispute started. Furthermore, another source of the agreement to submit the dispute between the investor and the host state to investment arbitration can be a BIT[148] or a MIT[149].

> **Example of an arbitration clause**
>
> Any controversy or claim arising out of or relating to this contract, or the breach thereof, shall be settled by arbitration administered by the [institution] under its [name of the arbitration rules]. The number of arbitrators shall be [one or three]. The language of the arbitration shall be [language] The place of arbitration shall be [city, State]. [Law of a particular jurisdiction] shall apply. Judgment on the award rendered by the arbitrator(s) may be entered in any court having jurisdiction thereof.

An arbitration clause is independent from an invalid contract, even if the clause is embodied in a contract (called *"doctrine of separability"* or *"separability principle"*). For example, if there is a dispute over the validity of a clause, the matter still goes to the arbitrators, and they decide if the clause is valid and if they have jurisdiction.[150]

---

[148] E.g., articles 7(2) and (3) od the BIT between South Africa and Zimbabwe from 2009: 7(2) If the dispute has not been settled within six (6) months from the date at which it was raised in writing, the dispute may at the choice of the investor, after notifying the party concerned of its intention to do so in writing, be submitted – (a) to the competent courts of the Party in whose territory the investment is made; (b) to arbitration by the International Centre for the Settlement of Investment Disputes (ICSID) established by the Convention on the Settlement of Investment Disputes between States and nationals of other States, opened for signature at Washington D.C./USA on March 18, 1965; or (c) an ad hoc arbitration tribunal, which unless otherwise agreed upon by the parties to the dispute, is to be established under the Arbitration Rules of the United Nationals Commission on International Trade Law (UNCITRAL). 7(3) If the investor submits the dispute to the competent court of the host Party or to international arbitration mentioned in sub-Article (2), the choice shall be final.

[149] E.g., article 26 of the ECT.

[150] See ALAN REDFERN/MARTIN HUNTER, Law and practice of international commercial arbitration (2005), pp. 164-165.

Prima Paint Corp. v. Flood & Conklin Mfg. Co.

388 U.S. 395 (1967)

Facts

The parties had entered into an agreement between the Prima Paint Corp. and and the Flood & Conklin Mfg. Co. regarding the latter's assets of its paint business. After the Prima Paint Corp. failed to make the first payment due under the agreement, the Flood & Conklin Mfg. Co. served notice to arbitrate. The Prima Paint Corp. filed suit seeking rescission of the entire agreement on the basis of fraud allegedly consisting of the Flood & Conklin Mfg. Co.'s misrepresentation that it was solvent and able to perform the agreement while it was completely insolvent. The Flood & Conklin Mfg. Co. moved to stay the court action pending arbitration. The Flood & Conklin Mfg. Co. contended that whether there was fraud in the inducement of the consulting agreement was a question for the arbitrators. The district court granted the Flood & Conklin Mfg. Co.'s motion with the court of appeals affirming.

In the following the Supreme Court held that

1. because the agreement was tied to the interstate transfer of the assets it affected interstate commerce and was within the coverage of the United States Arbitration Act of 1925. As the *"saving clause"* in § 2 of the United States Arbitration Act of 1925 indicates, the purpose of it was to make arbitration agreements as enforceable as other contracts.
2. the arbitration clause in the agreement was separable from the rest of the agreement; and
3. allegations as to the validity of the agreement in general, as opposed to the arbitration clause in particular, were to be decided by the arbitrator.

The Supreme Court held therefore, that a claim of fraud in the inducement of a contract containing an arbitration clause was subject to arbitration because the arbitration provision was severable from the rest of the agreement.

Buckeye Check Cashing Inc. v. Cardegna et al.

546 U.S. 440

The Court held with reference Prima Paint Corp. v. Flood & Conklin Mfg. Co. that regardless of whether a dispute is brought to federal or state court, a challenge to the validity of a contract as a whole, and not specifically to the arbitration clause within must go to the arbitrator and not to the court.

As a matter of substantive Federal arbitration law, an arbitration provision is severable from the remainder of the contract. Unless the challenge is to the arbitration clause itself, the issue of the contract's validity is considered by the arbitrator in the first instance.

4.1.2. Choice of the applicable law/substantive law

The *"choice-of-law"*-provision is often included in the arbitration clause, which can be found either in an investment contract, in a separate arbitration agreement between the parties, in a BIT or MIT.[151] In a choice of law provision the parties specify that any dispute arising under the contract shall be determined in accordance with the law of a particular jurisdiction. This may be some substantive national law (of one of the states which are contracting parties of the BIT, MIT or the law of a third state), national law including its private international law (conflicts of law) or even international law. The law of the contract (substantive law) is not the same as the law governing the arbitration.[152] The law governing the arbitration is the law governing the arbitration proceedings (*lex arbitri*) and in the absence of the agreement of the parties thereon, it would be determined by the arbitrators.

---

[151] Usually, the agreement to arbitrate takes the form of a clause within an investment contract. The arbitration agreement is a contract by its own and separable from the substantive contract in which it sits.

[152] See REDFERN/HUNTER, op. cit., p. 121 and FRIEDLAND, op. cit., p. 90.

4.1.3. Number of the arbitrators

An arbitration tribunal is a panel of one or more arbitrators. The parties to a dispute are usually free to agree on the number and composition of the arbitral tribunal or can even leave the number of arbitrators to the discretion of the institution.[153] In some legal systems, an arbitration clause which provides for two arbitrators (or any other even number) is understood to imply that the appointed arbitrators will select an additional arbitrator as a chairman of the tribunal, to avoid deadlock situations.

4.1.4. Choice of place (seat of arbitration)

The choice of the place of arbitration is one of the crucial aspects of every arbitration. The seat of arbitration does not have to be the place of the hearings which may be held at any location chosen by the arbitral tribunal; thereby the seat of arbitration does not alter (although usually the place of the arbitration is the same as the location of the hearings). Actually, it can be said that the seat of arbitration is the place (and thus the jurisdiction) to which the arbitration is tied.

The seat of arbitration determines which national mandatory rules would apply in the arbitration. Moreover, the seat of arbitration may also have impact on the applicable arbitration rules (provided that the parties have not agreed thereon). In addition, the seat of arbitration determines which courts would have supervisory powers over the arbitration and the extent of this supervision. Finally, the seat of arbitration may be very important in the enforcement process. Usually, the parties want to have arbitration in a place or state which is a contracting state of the *"New York Convention"*. Like this, they are sure that the award will be enforced (e.g., ICSID has its own *"enforcement scheme"*

---

[153] GARY B. BORN, International commercial arbitration, volume 1, (2009), p. 1360 and FRIEDLAND, op. cit., pp. 66 et seq.

and a member state of ICSID accepts that a tribunal decision is treated as a decision rendered by a domestic court).[154]

4.1.5. Choice of arbitration rules/procedural rules

There are samples for such clauses from arbitration institutions in which it is usually held that if the parties do not choose or regulate certain points, the rules of the chosen arbitration institutions have to be applied. For example, ICC Arbitration is possible only if there is an agreement between the parties providing for it. Furthermore, it is possible to choose also the comprehensive UNCITRAL Arbitration Rules. UNCITRAL itself does not have its own arbitration facilities, but its Arbitration Rules are adopted by many institutions, and widely accepted.[155] Many BIT or MIT do not make specific reference to particular rules, but provide for submission of disputes to a specific arbitration institution (e.g., ICSID); in those cases, the applicable arbitration rules are by default the rules of that institution, in force either at the time of entering into force of the BIT or MIT or at the time when the investment was made or at the time when the dispute between the state and the investor started.

Antoine Biloune and Marine Drive Complex, Ltd. v. Ghana Investments Centre and the Government of Ghana

95 ILR 184

Antoine Biloune, a Syrian national, made an investment agreement with the Ghana Investment Centre (which included an arbitration clause referring to the UNCITRAL Arbitration Rules) regarding the development of a hotel resort complex on "*Marine Drive*" in the city of Accra, Ghana. Before the completion of the hotel resort the government officials issued a stop-work order, citing the lack of building permit and the city government demolished part of the project. After receipt of evidence from the parties

---

[154] See also REDFERN/HUNTER, op. cit., p. 121 and FRIEDLAND, op. cit., pp. 64 et seq.

[155] See NIEK PETERS, The fundamentals of international commercial arbitration (2017), pp. 51 et seq.

and a hearing, the three judges arbitral panel issued an arbitral award. The arbitrators found the existence of a constructive expropriation by the Government of Ghana of Antoine Biloune's investment and awarded him the fair market value of the investment at the time of the expropriation, plus interest and cost.

Composition of the arbitral tribunal

The Ghanaian side did not appoint an arbitrator in order to frustrate the arbitration. In such a situation the UNCITRAL Arbitration Rules empower the General Secretary of the Permanent Court of Arbitration to designate an "*appointing authority*" to appoint the missing arbitrator.

Place of arbitration / language of arbitration

Since the parties had not otherwise agreed, the tribunal selected English as the language of the arbitration and designated Washington D.C., USA as the place of arbitration.

Jurisdiction over human rights claims

The tribunal held that it lacked the jurisdictional power under the arbitration clause to address the human rights claims. It limited its decision to the investment dispute which the parties had agreed to arbitrate. The human rights claims had to be brought to regular courts.

Applicable law

The arbitration agreement specified that the case should be construed according to the laws of Ghana. Because no party showed that Ghanaian law diverged from customary principles of international law, the central issue of expropriation was decided by the application of international law.

4.1.6. Language of arbitration

In arbitral proceedings the language of arbitration may be chosen by the parties, whereas in judicial proceedings the official language of the state, in which the competent court resides, will be automatically applied.[156]

4.2.   Request for arbitration and admission of the case

To commence an arbitration, the claimant needs to file its case according to the chosen arbitration rules by submitting a *"request for arbitration"* with the competent authority if the parties did not choose an ad hoc arbitration. After acknowledging receipt of a *"request"* and verifying its correspondence to the requirements, the secretariat will notify the respondent party or parties. It will also inform the claimant that it has done so, and indicate the date of receipt of the *"request"*. Very often the chosen arbitration rules require a particular form and content for the *"request"*, which has to be accompanied usually by a non-refundable advance payment, to cover administrative costs, and the required number of copies of the *"request"*. Furthermore, it is also expected from the claimant to appoint the arbitrator or to nominate the arbitrator for confirmation (if the applicable arbitration rules provide that the arbitrators would be appointed by the arbitral institution; e.g., as it is the case with ICC arbitration rules).[157]

4.3.   Appointment of the arbitrator/arbitrators

The arbitral tribunal usually consists of a sole arbitrator or a panel of three arbitrators. In latter case, each party appoints one arbitrator. The claimant does so in the request for arbitration, and the respondent appoints its arbitrator after receiving the *"request for arbitration"*. The arbitrators appointed by the parties shall appoint the third, presiding arbitrator. If the parties do not choose their arbitrators, then the competent authority will appoint the arbitrators usually from a list of suggested arbitrators according to the chosen arbitration rules. However, it is rare in international

---

[156]   See FRIEDLAND, op. cit., p. 70.
[157]   See YVES DERAINS/ERIC A. SCHWARTZ, A guide to the ICC rules of arbitration (2005), pp. 41 et seq. and MICHAEL MCILWRATH/JOHN SAVAGE, op. cit., p. 227.

investment disputes to entrust the appointment of the arbitrators to a national court.[158]

4.4.   Arbitration proceedings[159]

The precise course of the arbitration proceedings depends on the arbitration rules that are used. However, arbitration proceedings follow usually a general framework. Once the arbitral tribunal has been constituted, the secretariat transmits the file to each member of the arbitral tribunal. From that time on, the general management of the case shifts to the arbitral tribunal. The arbitral tribunal is responsible for running the proceeding and deciding on the merits of a dispute. Accordingly, the parties correspond directly with the arbitral tribunal, while sending copies of their correspondence and submissions also to the other parties. However, the secretariat monitors the arbitral process from start to finish, making sure that cases run smoothly and correctly. It reviews the progress of each case to ensure that it advances at the right speed and in line with the chosen arbitration rules. Furthermore, the arbitration rules provide that the arbitral tribunal can order interim or conservatory measures. Moreover, in the absence of an agreement between the parties as to the applicable rules of law, the arbitral tribunal applies the rules of law which it determines to be appropriate. Depending on the chosen arbitration rules, the parties and arbitrators are free to fix the rules of procedure, subject to any mandatory provisions that may be applicable. The parties may determine, for instance, whether and to what extent document production requests or cross-examination will be allowed. The arbitral tribunal proceeds in order to establish the facts of the case by all appropriate means. The parties have the right to be heard; the arbitral tribunal may also decide to hear witnesses and experts, and may summon any party to provide additional evidence. After the last hearing concerning matters to be decided in an

---

[158] See PETERS, op. cit., pp. 128 et seq. and JULIAN D. M. LEW/LOUKAS A. MISTELIS/STEFAN M. KRÖLL, Comparative international commercial arbitration (2003), p. 242.

[159] See also as an overview: https://iccwbo.org/dispute-resolution-services/arbitration/procedure/.

award or the filing of the last authorized submissions, the arbitral tribunal will declare the proceedings closed with respect to the matters to be decided in the award.

4.5. Arbitral award

After the closing of the proceedings, the arbitral tribunal will render its final decision and write an arbitral award that is signed by the arbitrators. It is deemed to be made at the place of the arbitration on the date it indicates. It is then notified to the parties.

4.6. Enforcement

Under the *"New York Convention of June 10, 1958 on the Recognition and Enforcement of Foreign Arbitral Awards"* (*"New York Convention"*) an arbitral award issued in a contracting state can generally be freely enforced in any other contracting state, only subject to certain, very limited defenses.

5. International Center for Settlement of Investment Disputes (ICSID)

5.1. Generally[160]

The International Centre for Settlement of Investment Disputes (ICSID), an institution of the World Bank, was founded in 1966 pursuant to the *"Convention on the Settlement of Investment Disputes between States and Nationals of Other States"* (the *"ICSID-Convention"*). In total 154 countries ratified the ICSID-Convention.

ICSID has an administrative council, chaired by the World Bank's President, and a secretariat. ICSID's headquarters are located in Washington D.C., USA. It provides facilities for the conciliation and arbitration of investment disputes between member countries and individual investors.

---

[160] See in general the information on the website: https://icsid.worldbank.org.

ICSID aims to facilitate investments to countries that need them the most and thus creates an investment dispute settlement system. The countries, which voluntarily ratify the convention, limit their sovereignty in order to encourage foreign investment. Thus, it is the only forum in the world, where a private individual or a legal entity can sue a state, because the states agreed to waive their state immunity.[161]

The ICSID-Convention provides the framework for the conduct of an arbitration proceeding. Furthermore, this framework is supplemented by detailed regulations and rules:

- *Rules of Procedure for the Institution of Conciliation and Arbitration Proceedings:*[162] The so-called *"Institution Rules"* explain how to institute an arbitration proceeding, including the form and contents of the request for arbitration. They apply to the steps taken between filing a request for arbitration until dispatch of the notice of registration.
- *Rules of Procedure for Arbitration Proceedings:*[163] The so-called *"Arbitration Rules"* govern the arbitration proceeding once a request for arbitration has been registered. They complement the ICSID-Convention procedural provisions, including provisions concerning post-award remedies.
- *Administrative and Financial Regulations*: The so-called *"Administrative and Financial Regulations"* contain provisions concerning the costs of the proceeding, publication of case-related information, functions with respect to individual proceedings, including the ICSID Secretariat's services, calculation of time limits and submission of supporting documentation, immunities and privileges; and official languages.

During the past decade, with the spread of BITs and MITs, which refer present and future investment disputes to the

---

[161] See AMAZU A. ASOZU, International commercial arbitration and African States: practice, participation and institutional development (2001), p. 388.

[162] See https://icsid.worldbank.org/en/Pages/icsiddocs/ICSID-Convention-Institution-Rules.aspx.

[163] See https://icsid.worldbank.org/en/Pages/icsiddocs/ICSID-Convention-Arbitration-Rules.aspx.

ICSID, the caseload of the ICSID has substantially increased. Up to 2018 ICSID has registered around 400 cases.

5.2. Specific aspects of an ICSID-Convention arbitration

5.2.1. Conditions for exercising ICSID-jurisdiction

Article 25 of the ICSID-Convention states the conditions for exercising ICSID-jurisdiction and requires three elements that have to be fulfilled:

(i)   Legal dispute arising out of an investment

According to article 25(1) of the ICSID-Convention an ICSID-arbitrator or tribunal can only arbitrate a legal dispute arising directly out of an investment. The convention has not defined the term *"legal dispute"* and *"investment"*. However, the term *"investment"* was discussed in the case ALCOA MINERALS OF JAMAICA V. JAMAICA,[164] where the tribunal held that a private company had invested substantial amounts in a foreign state in reliance upon an agreement with that state, and this contribution of capital was held to be one type of *"investment"*.

(ii)   Dispute between a contracting state and a national of another contracting state

Article 25(1) of the ICSID-Convention requires a dispute between a contracting state (or any constituent subdivision or agency of a contracting state designated to ICSID by that state) and a national of another contracting state:

– *Contracting state:* According to article 25(1) of the ICSID-Convention, the state and the investor's state must be *"contracting states"*.

---

[164] ALCOA V. JAMAICA CASE, CASE NO ARB/74/2, 4 Y.B. COM. ARB. 206 (1979).

- *Constituant subdivision or agency of a contracting state designated to ICSID by that state*: In order to be able to ask for an ICSID-Arbitration a constituent subdivision or agency has to be designated to ICSID.
- *National of another contracting state*: Article 25(2) of the ICSID-Convention defines a national of another contracting state as (a) any natural person who had the nationality of a contracting state other than the state party to the dispute on the date on which the parties consented to submit such dispute to conciliation or arbitration as well as on the date on which the request was registered according to the requirements of the ICSID-Convention, but does not include any person who on either date also had the nationality of the contracting state party to the dispute; and (b) any juridical person which had the nationality of a contracting state other than the state party to the dispute on the date on which the parties consented to submit such dispute to conciliation or arbitration and any juridical person which had the nationality of the contracting state party to the dispute on that date and which, because of foreign control, the parties have agreed should be treated as a national of another contracting state for the purposes of the ICSID-Convention.

(iii)   Consent to arbitration

Clear consent to arbitrate is critical for any arbitration. It is the cornerstone of the jurisdiction of ICSID. Article 25(1) of the ICSID-Convention limits the jurisdiction of ICSID to cases where both parties have specifically consented to submit their dispute to ICSID. Thus, two written consents are necessary:

- *Consent by the state to the ICSID-Convention:* Consenting to the ICISD-Convention alone does not mean that the state agrees to all arbitration. A state's ratification of the ICSID-Convention does not obligate that state nor private individuals or legal entities of that state to use the ICSID-centre's facilities for the resolution of investment disputes.

- *Consent in individual contract, BIT or MIT:* The state and the investor both must consent to ICSID-arbitration with respect to a given contract or dispute.

Examples of ICISD-arbitration clauses[165]

A.   Consent in respect of future disputes

Under the convention, consent may be given in advance, with respect to a defined class of future disputes. Clauses relating to future disputes are a common feature of investment agreements between contracting states and investors who are nationals of other contracting states.

"The [Government]/[name of constituent subdivision or agency] of name of Contracting State (hereinafter the Host state) and name of investor (hereinafter the Investor) hereby consent to submit to the International Centre for Settlement of Investment Disputes (hereinafter the Centre) any dispute arising out of or relating to this agreement for settlement by [conciliation]/[arbitration]/[conciliation followed, if the dispute remains unresolved within time limit of the communication of the report of the Conciliation Commission to the parties, by arbitration] pursuant to the Convention on the Settlement of Investment Disputes between States and Nationals of Other States (hereinafter the Convention)."

B.   Consent in respect of existing disputes

Consent may also be given in respect of a particular, existing dispute:

"The [Government]/[name of constituent subdivision or agency] of name of Contracting State (hereinafter the Host State) and name of investor (hereinafter the Investor) hereby consent to submit to the International Centre for Settlement of Investment Disputes (hereinafter the Centre) for settlement by [conciliation]/[arbitration]/[conciliation followed, if the dispute remains unresolved within time limit of the communication of the report of the Conciliation Commission to the parties, by arbitration] pursuant to the

---

[165]   See http://icsidfiles.worldbank.org/icsid/icsid/staticfiles/model-clauses-en/7.htm.

Convention on the Settlement of Investment Disputes between States and Nationals of Other States, the following dispute arising out of the investment described below: ..."

The parties' consent necessarily includes their agreement to abide by the ICSID-Convention, the Arbitration Rules, and to the extent permitted by the aforementioned convention and the rules, any modifications thereto agreed by the parties.

Amco Asia Corporation, Pan American Development Limited, P.T. Amco Indonesia v Republic of Indonesia

ICSID Award, AMCO Asia Corp. et al. v. The Republic of Indonesia, YCA 1992, at 73 et seq.

In 1968, Amco Asia, a United States corporation, contracted with P.T. Wisma Kartika (P.T. Wisma), an Indonesian real estate company, to construct and manage a hotel on P.T. Wisma's land. Amco Asia was to receive a percentage of the profits from the hotel's operations. In accordance with Indonesian law, Amco Asia was issued a foreign investment license which required Amco Asia to invest fresh foreign equity capital in the project and which entitled Amco Asia to receive tax and other benefits. The license contained an ICSID-arbitration clause. When the license was approved, Amco Asia formed P.T. Amco, an Indonesian company as subsidiary, and assigned its rights under the contract to P.T. Amco. In 1980 a dispute arose, Amco's foreign investment license was revoked and Amco Asia commenced ICSID-arbitration raising several claims.

Two issues regarding the *"jurisdiction"* are important in this case:

1. Consent of the Parties, and
2. Nationality

1)   Consent of the Parties

Indonesia said that it did not agree to an ICSID-arbitration, although they joined the ICSID-Convention. Art. 25(1) of the ICSID-Convention requires the written consent of the parties to arbitrate their dispute, and the fact that Indonesia did join ICSID, is not enough to create jurisdiction.

The tribunal held that there was consent to the ICSID-arbitration. This case demonstrated, however, that written consent need not to be embodied in an investment contract, nor in a single instrument, and may be expressed in two or more documents like in investment codes, laws or BITs, wherein a state agrees to arbitration.

2)   Nationality

Indonesia disagreed that the parties had consented to treat P.T. Amco as being under foreign control and contended that Amco Asia and Pan American, although foreign corporations, were not parties to the agreement that included the ICSID arbitration clause. Indonesia asserted that P.T. Amco has not to be considered as a national of another state under Article 25(2)(b) of the ICSID-Convention and, therefore, could not assert a right to ICSID-arbitration.

The tribunal however held that the parties did agree to treat P.T. Amco as a foreign national and Amco Asia and Pan American as parties to the ICSID-arbitration. The Tribunal observed that the concept of nationality in ICSID was a *"classical one, based on the law under which the juridical person has been incorporated, the place of incorporation and the place of the social seat."* The tribunal then adopted a less stringent test for finding the foreign corporation nationality. It held that *"What is needed ... is 1° that the juridical person, party to the dispute be legally a national of the Contracting State which is the other party, and 2° that this juridical person being under foreign control, to the knowledge of the Contracting State, the parties agrees to treat it as a foreign juridical person."*

The tribunal found that Indonesia agreed to treat P.T. Amco as a foreign national when Indonesia approved the investment license application (and the ICSID clause in it). Furthermore, the tribunal explained that by approving the application referring to a *"foreign business"* it was *"crystal clear that [Indonesia] agreed to treat P.T. Amco as a national of another Contracting State, for the purpose of the Convention."* Moreover, it added that *"[t]here is no provision in the Convention imposing a formal indication, in the arbitration clause itself, of the nationality of the foreign juridical or natural persons who control the juridical person having the nationality of the Contracting state, party to the dispute."*

5.2.2 Enforcement

An ICSID-arbitral award is binding for the parties. Thus, such an award is equal to a domestic decision with regard to its enforcement. The ICSID member states are obliged by international law to enforce such an arbitral award. As the ICSID-Convention is an international treaty, the states would violate international public law if they do not enforce an ICSID-award (article 53 of the ICSID-Convention).

Furthermore, according to article 54 of the ICSID-Convention each party agrees to accept the arbitral award. As a result, arbitral awards of an ICSID-Convention are considered to be final and binding, and may not be set aside by the courts of any contracting state.

5.2.3. Post award remedies

In order to ensure the finality, ICSID arbitral awards are binding on the disputing parties, may not be appealed, and are not subject to any remedies except those provided for in the convention (article 53 of the ICSID-Convention). However, challenges to an ICSID-award must be brought within the framework of the ICSID-Convention and pursuant to its provisions. The choice of remedies offered reflects a deliberate election by the drafters of the convention to ensure finality of awards. Thus, the ICSID-Convention provides for several possible remedies after an award has been rendered. These are:

- *Supplementation and rectification*: Article 49(2) of the ICSID-Convention provides a remedy for omissions and errors in the award. Supplementation and rectification can only be made by the tribunal that rendered the award.
- *Interpretation*: Article 50 of the ICSID-Convention deals with disputes between parties to arbitration proceedings relating to the interpretation of the award. The

interpretation will be given, if possible, by the tribunal that rendered the award. If this is not possible, a new tribunal will be constituted for this purpose.

- *Revision*: Article 51 of the ICSID-Convention deals with revision, which is a substantive alteration of the original award on the basis of newly discovered facts that were unknown when the award was rendered. Any revision shall be made, if possible, by the same tribunal that rendered the award. If this is not possible, a new tribunal will be constituted for this purpose.
- *Annulment*: Article 52 of the ICSID-Convention foresees the annulment of an award under certain narrowly defined circumstances. Annulment proceedings always take place before a separate ad hoc committee.

The only way to annul fully or partially an award is pursuant to one or more of the five specific grounds provided by article 52 of the ICSID-Convention.

On these grounds, it is possible to set out the arbitration award:

- The tribunal was not properly constituted (article 52(1)(a) ICSID-Convention; e.g., there was an error in appointing an arbitrator),
- The tribunal exceeded manifestly its powers (article 52(1)(b) ICSID-Convention),
- Corruption (article 52(1)(c) ICSID-Convention (e.g., one, several or all members were bribed),
- Serious departure from a fundamental rule of procedure (article 52(1)(d) ICSID-Convention), and
- Award did not state the reasons it was based on (article 52(1)(e) ICSID-Convention).

Except for the ground of corruption, the parties have to initiate the process in article 52 of the ICSID-Convention within a certain time period.

Klöckner Industrie-Anlagen GmbH and others v. United Republic of Cameroon and Société Camerounaise des Engrais

ICSID Case No. ARB/81/2; 2 ICSID Reports 95

Klöckner Industrie-Anlagen GmbH, a German multinational group, was contracted to build and operate a fertilizer factory in Cameroon. Société Camerounaise des Engrais

(SOCAME), a Cameroonian joint venture in which Klöckner Industrie-Anlagen GmbH owned 51 percent and Cameroon 49 percent, was to operate the factory. Among the various contracts concluded for the project was a so-called "*Establishment Agreement*" in which Cameroon gave SOCAME benefits including favorable tax and customs treatment. The "*Establishment Agreement*" also contained an ICSID-arbitration clause. SOCAME's capacity to appear as a party in the proceeding, however, was challenged on the basis, *inter alia*, that it was not a foreign company (or designated as one), but rather a Cameroonian.

Klöckner requested an annulment of the arbitral award on three grounds, based on Article 52(1)(b), (d) and (e) ICSID-Convention, because:

1. the tribunal has manifestly exceeded its powers;
2. there has been a serious departure from a fundamental rule of procedure; and
3. the award has failed to state the reasons on which it was based.

The ad hoc committee annulled the award finding that the tribunal failed to apply the proper law, without proving its existence or attempting to identify the rules which form the context of the principle, and then exceeded its powers.

Scrutinizing the quality of the award of the tribunal by the ad hoc committee attracted criticism.

The dispute was resubmitted to a second tribunal two months later, and the tribunal awarded Klöckner Industrie-Anlagen GmbH the balance of the purchase price, and awarded Cameroon damages. Against the request by both parties for annulment of the second award, the second ad hoc committee rejected both requests for annulment.

Maritime International Nominees Establishment v. Republic of Guinea

ICSID Case No. ARB/84/4; 4 ICSID Reports 79

Maritime International Nominees Establishment (MINE) and the government of Guinea established a joint venture company called SOTRAMAR to transport of bauxite, but the government concluded a contract with another company to transport of bauxite. Upon filing by MINE at ICSID-arbitration, the tribunal decided that Guinea breached the contract with MINE, preventing SOTRAMAR from performing the contract, and awarded damages considering lost profits to MINE.

Guinea requested partial annulment of the award, based on Article 52(1)(b), (d) and (e) ICSID-Convention, because:

1. the tribunal has manifestly exceeded its powers;
2. there has been a serious departure from a fundamental rule of procedure; and
3. the award has failed to state the reasons on which it is based.

The ad hoc committee annulled the award as to the amount of damages. After MINE resubmitted to the new tribunal for decision on damages, the parties agreed to settle the case.

The ad hoc committee explained one of the requirements of annulment of *"excess of powers and proper law"* from the viewpoint of the party autonomy that grants the parties unlimited freedom to agree on the rules of law applicable to the substance of their dispute and requires the tribunal to respect the parties' autonomy and to apply those rules. A tribunal's disregard of the agreed rules of law would constitute derogation from the terms of reference within which the tribunal has been authorized to function. If the derogation is manifest, it entails a manifest excess of power.

The ad hoc committee annulled the award as to the amount of damages holding that the award must state the reasons on which it is based. The requirement to state the reasons as it is defined in Article 52 (1)(e) is to explain how and why the tribunal came to its decision. It is satisfied as long as the award enables one to follow how the tribunal proceeded from Point A to Point B, and eventually to its conclusion, even if it made an error of fact or of law.

6. Recognition and enforcement of arbitral awards

6.1. Generally[166]

The *"New York Convention of June 10, 1958 on the Recognition and Enforcement of Foreign Arbitral Awards"*

---

[166] See for general information: http://www.newyorkconvention.org/.

(the *"New York Convention"*) is one of the key instruments in international arbitration.

Basically, the New York Convention requires courts of each contracting state to:

- recognize an international arbitration agreement in writing and to refuse to allow a dispute to be litigated before them when it is subject to an arbitration agreement (article II of the New York Convention); and
- recognize and enforce foreign arbitral awards (article III of the New York Convention).

Thus, the New York Convention does not know any requirements with regard to the nationality of the parties. It is only required that the arbitral award comes from a contracting state of the aforesaid convention.

As of January 2019, the New York Convention has 159 state parties, which includes 156 of the 193 United Nations member states plus the Cook Islands, the Holy See, and the State of Palestine.

6.2.   Reciprocal treatment

Many states have made a reservation regarding the New York Convention as they will apply the convention only to the extent to which a reciprocal treatment is granted by other states: *"When signing, ratifying or acceding to this Convention, or notifying extension under article X hereof, any State may on the basis of reciprocity declare that it will apply the Convention to the recognition and enforcement of awards made only in the territory of another Contracting State."* (article I(3) of the New York Convention).[167]

6.3.   Referring to arbitration

The court of a contracting state, when seized of an action in a matter in respect of which the parties have made a written arbitration agreement, shall, at the request of one of the

---

[167] See the list of declarations and reservations on the following website: http://www.newyorkconvention.org/list+of+contracting+states.

parties, refer the parties to arbitration, unless it finds that the said agreement is null and void, inoperative or incapable of being performed (article II(3) of the New York Convention).

6.4. Enforcement of awards

The party who victories in the arbitration typically goes to a domestic court seeking recognition and enforcement of the award. The party has to file a motion together with the duly authenticated original award or a duly certified copy thereof and the original written agreement or a duly certified copy thereof (also translated in the respective language by a sworn translator or by a diplomatic or consular agent; see also article IV of the New York Convention). Usually, such a *"recognition and enforcement procedure"* can be made anywhere the losing party has assets, and where the New York Convention is applicable law. The domestic court has to enforce the arbitral award as it would enforce its own decisions.

6.5. Defenses to enforcement

Article V of the New York Convention regulates in what situation a domestic court is able to refuse to enforce a decision of an arbitration tribunal. There is a list of the defenses in article V(1) of the New York Convention that may be raised in opposition to the confirmation of an award:

- the parties were under some incapacity, or the agreement is not valid under the law,
- the party against whom the award is invoked was not given proper notice of appointment of the arbitrator or the arbitration proceedings,
- the award deals with a difference not contemplated by the terms of the arbitration, or it contains decisions on matters beyond the scope of the arbitration,
- the composition of the arbitral authority or procedure was not in accordance with the parties' agreement, or
- the award is not yet binding or was set aside by a competent authority of the country in which the award was made.

Furthermore, recognition and enforcement may be refused:

- if the subject matter of the difference is not capable of settlement by arbitration, or
- if recognition or enforcement of the award is contrary to public policy of the country in which enforcement is sought (Article V(2) of the New York Convention).

Should the domestic court refuse to enforce an arbitral award for one of the reasons stated in Article V of the New York Convention, then it does not annul the arbitral award as it had just to decide with regard a defense against recognition and enforcement.

Parsons & Whittemore Overseas Co. v. Société Générale de L'Industrie du Papier (RAKTA)

US Court of Appeals Second Circuit, 508 F.2nd 969

Parsons & Whittemore Overseas (*"Overseas"*), an American corporation, and Société Générale de L'Industrie du Papier (*"RAKTA"*), an Egyptian corporation, entered in a contract for the construction and operation of a paper mill in Egypt. The contract provided for arbitration under the Rules of the International Chamber of Commerce (*"ICC Rules"*). RAKTA initiated arbitration proceedings claiming damages for breach of the contract, and a final award was rendered in its favor. The award was confirmed by United States federal district court. Overseas appealed this decision and argued that: (i) the enforcement of the award would violate US public policy; (ii) the award represents a decision on matters not appropriate for arbitration; (iii) the Arbitral Tribunal denied Overseas an adequate opportunity to present its case; (iv) the award is predicated upon the resolution of issues outside the scope of the contractual agreement for arbitration, and (v) the award is in manifest disregard of the law.

The United States Court of Appeals for the Second Circuit confirmed the district court's decision and confirmed the award. In dismissing the first objection, the Court of Appeals held that the public policy provision of Article V(2)(b) of the New York Convention should be construed narrowly, and the enforcement of foreign arbitral awards may be denied only where enforcement would violate the forum state's most basic notions of morality and justice.

101

The court also ruled that the arbitrability of the claim, pursuant to Article V(2)(a) of the New York Convention, was not affected by the fact that United States foreign policy was somehow implicated in the dispute. The court found no violation of due process under Article V(1)(b) of the New York Convention and found no excess of the Tribunal's jurisdiction under Article V(1)(c) of the New York Convention. Finally, the court declined to determine whether there was an implied defense of *"manifest disregard of the law"* under the New York Convention, instead holding that even if there was such a defense, Overseas had failed to establish it.

6.6. Attachment prior to the enforcement of international arbitral awards

The issue of whether attachment of property belonging to a party should be permitted prior to the completion of arbitration is debatable. Several court decisions dealt with this question under the New York Convention.

Cooper v. Ateliers de la Motobecane

S.A., 57 N.Y.2d 408, 442 N.E.2d 1239, 456 N.Y.S.2d 728 (1982)

The New York Court of Appeals has held that attachment is impermissible pending arbitral proceedings in commercial disputes under the New York Convention.

Carolina Power & Light Co. v. Uranex

451 F Supp. 1044

In a dispute involving an American and a French Company, the court reached a contrary decision to the aforementioned case. It held that there was nothing to prevent the plaintiff from commencing the action by attachment if such procedure is available under the applicable law.

However, in abstraction of these American court decisions various legislative and judicial bodies of other signatory countries to the New York Convention (e.g., Austria, Belgium, Denmark, England and Wales, France, Germany,

Switzerland) as well as major arbitration rule-setting bodies (e.g., UNCITRAL Arbitration Rules) allow a prior attachment.

VII. Intellectual property protection and transfer of technology to developing countries

1. Generally

Foreign investments are crucial for the economic development as they strengthen the domestic research and development and entail a know-how transfer. Additionally, the resulting trade allows a host state to acquire high value-added goods through importation that are necessary in order to obtain a better economic development for which the developing countries pay with their natural resources and the surplus of labor. Along with the transfer of technology to the host states, which are evidently to the benefit of the latter, goes the need of the foreign investors that their intellectual property rights are protected in the developing countries.[168]

For centuries, intellectual property rights have been matters of national concern. Nearly each state had its own intellectual property regime based on the national needs and priorities. At the end of the 19 century, the idea of a harmonization of intellectual property law came up and in the following decades several conventions[169] have been adopted in order to establish general standards of protection.[170]

Thus, it became for the foreign investors, which were very often also the owners of intellectual property rights, easier to protect these rights in various countries. Nevertheless, foreign investors had to know the domestic law and to file nationally for registration of their intellectual property rights. Furthermore, depending on the actual legislation they had to maintain their rights actively, otherwise they were risking to lose them.

---

[168] See SORNARAJAH, International law, p. 44.
[169] The first major international legal instrument is the Paris Convention for the Protection of Industrial Property from 1883.
[170] IAN INKSTER, Intellectual property, information and divergences in economic development – institutional patterns and outcomes circa 1421–2000, in: The role of intellectual property rights in biotechnology innovation, edited by David Castle, pp. 416 et seq.

McDonald's Corporation v. Joburgers Drive-Inn Restaurant (PTY) LTD

In the Supreme Court of South Africa, 1996

Case No. 547/95, 1996.

Facts

McDonald's had obtained registration of its trademarks in South Africa through applications in the years 1968, 1974, 1979, 1980, 1984, and 1985. However, McDonald's decided in 1986 not to open franchises in South Africa as a protest against South Africa's policy of apartheid. Because of this decision, McDonald's did not actively maintain its trademarks in South Africa. In 1993, Mr. Sombonos, a wealthy South African restaurateur, applied for trademark protection for the McDonald's name and other formerly protected McDonald's trademarks. At the same time, Mr. Sombonos sought the expungement of all of McDonald's trademarks. Mr. Sombonos intended to change the name of his Joburger restaurants to McDonald's, to advertise his restaurants with the "*Golden Arches*", and to serve "*Big Macs*" and "*Egg McMuffins*". The McDonald's Corporation, wanting to establish new franchises in South Africa, filed cross-claims against Mr. Sombonos claiming that he was infringing McDonald's trademarks. McDonald's alleged that South African trademark law did not require the active maintenance of trademarks if "*special circumstances*" prevented a company from doing so, and they further contended that the South African trademark act of 1993 provided for the "*protection of 'well known' marks emanating from certain foreign countries*" (Section 35).

Trial Court

The case was heard at the trial court level in late 1995. Surprisingly, the trial court found in favor of Mr. Sombonos, and thus granted trademark protection for the McDonald's name to him, and called for the expungement of all other trademarks of the McDonald's corporation. The trial court held that McDonald's 1986 decision not to do business in South Africa (because of the apartheid) was not a "*special circumstance*" that excused them from regularly maintaining their trademarks and thus, they lost any right for protection. The trial court further held that the McDonald's trade name was not *"well known"* throughout all of South Africa and was thus not afforded protection under the *"well known marks application"* of the 1993 trademark act. The trial court relied heavily on a market survey indicating that the name was, in fact, not well known. Interestingly, the trial court was not swayed by the fact that this market survey was conducted primarily on South African blacks, who were generally poor, had no access to television, and had, until recently, not been allowed to leave the country. McDonald's appealed the decision.

Appellate Court

In September of 1996, the appellate court reversed the trial court's decision, and granted trademark protection to the McDonald's Corporation. The court concluded that the McDonald's name was well known throughout South Africa, and was thus entitled to trademark protection under the 1993 trademark act. In so ruling, the court relied on market surveys of white South Africans that showed that the McDonald's name was recognized by 90% of the white population. Furthermore, the court noted that the white population would be the primary customers and franchisees of the McDonald's Corporation, and was therefore the appropriate population for market surveys testing for recognition of the McDonald's name (the court also noted that the lack of recognition among South African blacks was caused by the previous apartheid system – the very system that prompted McDonald's not to do business in South Africa in 1986). Moreover, the court also grounded its decision on the belief that Mr. Sombonos would not have gone through such time and expense to secure the McDonald's name if he was not convinced of its great value.

However, over the years developing countries were pressured to strengthen the national intellectual property rights in their domestic laws in order to harmonize them with those of developed countries.[171]

---

[171] See RUTH OKEDIJI, New treaty development and harmonization of intellectual property law, in: Trading in knowledge, development

106

Thus, in the last decades there have been changes in the international legal and trade structures in the field of the intellectual property rights. Since 1980, new technologies stimulated and pushed for new standards of intellectual property protection. In 1994, the World Trade Organization's (WTO) Agreement on Trade-Related Aspects of Intellectual Property Rights (TRIPS) as well as its amendments provided a minimum standard of protection of intellectual property around the world, which each WTO member state has to provide, brought common international rules, and created a dispute resolution system to challenge breaches of these standards. The increase of bilateral, regional and international free trade agreements included also elements of intellectual property rights, implemented the minimum standards of TRIPS.[172]

2. International organizations

Mainly two international organizations help promoting the protection of intellectual property throughout the world.

2.1. World Intellectual Property Organization (WIPO)[173]

The World Intellectual Property Organization (WIPO) was created in 1967 as the successor of the former BIRPI (*"Bureaux Internationaux Réunis pour la Protection de la Propriété Intellectuelle"*) and has its headquarter in Geneva, Switzerland.

It was formally created by the *"Convention Establishing the World Intellectual Property Organization"*, which makes the

---

perspectives on TRIPS, trade and sustainability, edited by Christophe Bellmann/Graham Dutfield/Ricardo Meléndez-Ortiz (2003), p. 90.

[172] See MARK J. DAVISON/ANN L. MONOTTI/LEANNE WISEMAN, Australian intellectual property law (2016), p. 13 and TANIA VOON, The world trade organization, the TRIPS agreement and traditional knowledge: in: Indigenous intellectual property, a handbook of contemporary research, edited by Matthew (2015), pp. 65 et seq.

[173] See https://www.wipo.int/about-wipo/en/history.html.

WIPO responsible for administering about 26 conventions and international agreements, *inter alia* the previously mentioned *"International Convention for the Protection of Industrial Property"* (*"Paris Convention"*), the *"Berne Convention for the Protection of Literary and Artistic Works"* (*"Berne Convention"*) and the *"Madrid Agreement Concerning the International Registration of Marks"* (*"Madrid Agreement"*) / *"Protocol Relating to the Madrid Agreement"* (*"Madrid Protocol"*).

> **Agreement between the United Nations and the World Intellectual Property Organization of 1974**
>
> Article 1 of the aforementioned agreement states: *"The United Nations recognizes the World Intellectual Property Organization ... as a specialized agency and as being responsible for taking appropriate action in accordance with its basic instrument, treaties and agreements administered by it, inter alia, for promoting creative intellectual activity and for facilitating the transfer of technology related to industrial property to the developing countries in order to accelerate economic, social and cultural development, subject to the competence and responsibilities of the United Nations and its organs..."*

2.2. Council for Trade-Related Aspects of Intellectual Property Rights (Council for TRIPs)[174]

The Council for Trade-Related Aspects of Intellectual Property Rights (Council for TRIPs) was created in 1995 with the adoption of the Agreement Establishing the World Trade Organization (WTO Agreement). As an organ of WTO it is responsible for administering the Agreement on Trade-Related Aspects of Intellectual Property Rights (TRIPs) and monitoring the operation of this agreement, in particular, member states' compliance with it. The Council for TRIPs has to consult the member states on matters relating to the trade-related aspects of intellectual property rights and provide any assistance requested by them in the context of dispute settlement procedures.

---

[174] See https://www.wto.org/english/tratop_e/trips_e/intel6_e.htm.

3.   Intellectual property treaties

Most matters relating to intellectual property rights are regulated internationally by multilateral treaties.

3.1.   International Convention for Protection of Industrial Property (Paris Convention)[175]

The International Convention for Protection of Industrial Property, usually known as the Paris Convention, adopted originally in 1883 and subsequently revised and amended on several occasions, applies to industrial property in the widest sense, including patents, trademarks, industrial designs, utility models, service marks, trade names, geographical indications and the repression of unfair competition. This international agreement was the first major step taken to help creators to ensure that their intellectual works were protected in other countries. There are nowadays in total 177 contracting parties to this convention.

---

[175]   See https://www.wipo.int/treaties/en/ip/paris/summary_paris.html.

Three basic principles are incorporated in the convention:

- *National treatment*: The provisions on national treatment require member states to give the same protection of industrial property to the nationals of other states that it grants to its own nationals.
- *Right of priority*: The convention provides for the right of priority in the case of patents (and utility models where they exist), marks and industrial designs. This right means that, based on a regular first application filed in one of the member states, the applicant may, within a certain period of time (12 months for patents and utility models; 6 months for industrial designs and marks), apply for protection in any of the other member states. These subsequent applications will be regarded as if they had been filed on the same day as the first application. In other words, they will have priority (therefore the expression *"right of priority"*) over applications filed by others during the said period of time for the same invention, utility model, mark or industrial design.
- *Common rules*: The convention lays down a few common rules, which set minimum standards that all member states must follow. The most important are:
  - a member state may not deny protection to industrial property because the work incorporating an invention was not manufactured in that state,
  - member states must protect trade names without requiring registration,
  - member states must outlaw false labeling (i.e., any indication that falsely identifies the source of goods, or the trader or manufacturer), and
  - each member state is required to take *"effective"* measures to prevent unfair competitions.

3.2. Berne Convention for the Protection of Literary and Artistic Property (Berne Convention)[176]

The Berne Convention for the Protection of Literary and Artistic Works, usually known as the Berne Convention, is an international agreement governing copyright, which was

---

[176] See https://www.wipo.int/treaties/en/ip/berne/summary_berne.html.

first accepted in Berne, Switzerland, in 1886, which was revised and amended on several occasions. This convention deals with the protection of works and the rights of their authors and establishes a *"union"* of states that is responsible for protecting artistic rights. Nowadays there are 176 states that are parties to the Berne Convention.

The convention is based on three basic principles and contains a series of provisions determining the minimum protection to be granted, as well as special provisions available to developing countries that want to make use of them.

The three basic principles are the following:

— *Principle of national treatment*: Works originating in one of the member states, i.e., works the author of which is a national of such a state or works first published in such a state) must be given the same protection in each of the other contracting states as the latter grants to the works of its own nationals.
— *Principle of "automatic" protection*: The member states are required to provide the same protection without any additional formalities. However, the country of origin can make the protection conditional of the author's first making an application for registration, or registering the work, or reserving rights in a contract of sale, or a similar condition.
— *Principle of "independence" of protection*: Protection is independent of the existence of protection in the country of origin of the work. However, if a member state provides for a longer term of protection than the minimum prescribed by the convention and the work ceases to be protected in the country of origin, protection may be denied once protection in the country of origin ceases.

The principle of common rules establishes minimum standards for granting copyrights common to all member states. The most important are:

— protection must include every production in the literary, scientific and artistic domain, whatever the mode or form of its expression,
— exclusive rights of authorization are the right to translate, the right to make adaptations and arrangements of the

work, the right to perform in public dramatic, dramatic-musical and musical works, the right to recite literary works in public, the right to communicate to the public the performance of such works, the right to broadcast, the right to make reproductions in any manner or form, and the right to use the work as a basis for an audio-visual work,

- the convention provides for *"moral rights"*, which is the right to claim authorship of the work and the right to object to any mutilation, deformation or other modification of, or other derogatory action in relation to, the work that would be prejudicial to the author's honour or reputation, and
- protection must be granted until the expiration of the 50th year after the author's death. There are, however, exceptions to this general rule. In the case of anonymous or pseudonymous works, the term of protection expires 50 years after the work has been lawfully made available to the public, except if the pseudonym leaves no doubt as to the author's identity or if the author discloses his or her identity during that period; in the latter case, the general rule applies. In the case of audio-visual (cinematographic) works, the minimum term of protection is 50 years after the making available of the work to the public (*"release"*) or – failing such an event – from the creation of the work. In the case of works of applied art and photographic works, the minimum term is 25 years from the creation of the work.

3.3.   Madrid System for the International Registration of Marks[177]

The legal basis for the Madrid System for the International Registration of Marks are the:

- Multilateral treaty Madrid Agreement Concerning the International Registration of Marks, which was concluded in 1891 and entered into force in 1892, subsequently revised several times, and

---

[177] See https://www.wipo.int/madrid/en/.

- Protocol Relating to the Madrid Agreement, which was concluded in 1989 and came into operation in 1996.

The aforementioned agreement as well as the protocol were adopted at diplomatic conferences held in Madrid, Spain. As of today, there are more than 100 members to the *"Madrid Union"*, covering 118 countries. These members represent more than 80% of the world trade, with potential for expansion as membership grows.

The Madrid system is the primary international system for facilitating the registration of trademarks in many states around the world as a trademark owner did not have to register his trademark in every state and thus it provides a centrally administered system, with which it is possible to obtain a bundle of single jurisdiction trademark registrations based on an *"international application"*. Once the WIPO receives an international application, it carries out an examination for compliance with the requirements of the legal basis of the *"Madrid System"*. If there are no irregularities in the application, the WIPO records the trademark in the *"International Register"*, publishes the international registration in the WIPO Gazette of International Marks, and forwards the application to the designated countries for examination pursuant to their domestic law. Unless a designated country acts within one year in order to refuse protection, the trademark is deemed protected. An international registration is effective for 10 years. It may be renewed for further periods of 10 years on payment of the prescribed fees.

The trademark owner may then extend the protection afforded to the international registration to one or more member jurisdictions, a process known as *"designation"*. A useful feature of the Madrid system is that this protection may generally be extended to additional jurisdictions at any time, such that international trademark protection can be extended to new jurisdictions, which subsequently join Madrid system, or to such other jurisdictions as the trademark owner may choose.

3.4. Agreement on Trade-Related Aspects of Intellectual Property Rights (TRIPS Agreement / TRIPS)[178]

The Agreement on Trade-Related Aspects of Intellectual Property Rights (TRIPS Agreement / TRIPS) is an annex to the Agreement Establishing the World Trade Organization (WTO) and thus TRIPS is administered by the WTO. It was negotiated at the end of the Uruguay Round of the General Agreement on Tariffs and Trade (GATT) in 1994. The TRIPS sets minimum standard for many forms of intellectual property regulation with a multilateral and comprehensive set of rights and obligations as applied to nationals of other WTO member states.

The areas of intellectual property that it covers are:

– copyright and related rights (i.e., the rights of performers, producers of sound recordings and broadcasting organizations),
– trademarks including service marks,
– geographical indications including appellations of origin; industrial designs,
– patents including the protection of new varieties of plants,
– the layout-designs of integrated circuits, and
– undisclosed information including trade secrets and test data.

The common minimum standard is given force in the following ways.

– TRIPS requires the WTO member states that the substantive obligations of the main conventions of the WIPO, the Paris Convention and the Berne Convention in their most recent versions, must be complied with. With the exception of the provisions of the Berne Convention on moral rights, all the main substantive provisions of these conventions are incorporated by reference and thus become obligations under the TRIPS Agreement between TRIPS member countries.
– The TRIPS Agreement fills in the gaps in many of the aforementioned conventions. Thus, TRIPS adds a

---

[178] See https://www.wto.org/english/tratop_e/trips_e/intel2_e.htm.

substantial number of additional obligations on matters where the pre-existing conventions are silent or were seen as being inadequate. The TRIPS Agreement is sometimes referred to as a Berne and Paris-plus agreement.

- The TRIPS Agreement lays down certain general principles applicable to all intellectual property rights enforcement procedures. Furthermore, it contains provisions on civil and administrative procedures and remedies, provisional measures, special requirements related to border measures and criminal procedures, which specify, in a certain amount of detail, the procedures and remedies that must be available so that right holders can effectively enforce their rights.
- Dispute settlement is governed by the TRIPS Agreement, which makes disputes between WTO Members about the respect of the TRIPS obligations subject to the WTO's dispute settlement procedures.
- The TRIPS Agreement operates with special transition periods for its implementation. The obligations under TRIPS apply equally to all member States, however developing countries were allowed extra time to implement the applicable changes to their national laws, in two tiers of transition according to their level of development. The transition period for developing countries expired in 2005. The transition period for least developed countries to implement TRIPS was extended to 2013, and until January 1, 2016 for pharmaceutical patents, with the possibility of further extension.
- The TRIPS Agreement provides for certain basic principles, such as national and most-favoured-nation treatment, and some general rules to ensure that procedural difficulties in acquiring or maintaining intellectual property rights do not nullify the substantive benefits that should flow from the Agreement. The obligations under the Agreement will apply equally to all member States, but developing countries will have a longer period to phase them in.

In addition to the minimum standards with regard to intellectual property rights created by the TRIPS agreement, many states have engaged in bilateral agreements to adopt a higher standard of protection. These agreements are also known as TRIPS+ or TRIPS-Plus.

4.   Technology transfer

Technology is only of value if there is a solid intellectual property protection. As we have seen, the technology of an investor is not just protected by intellectual property rights in his home state, but also in the host state as nowadays, nearly all developing countries adopted at least minimum standards. Furthermore, cross border investments are an important means of transferring technology to developing countries. Usually, technology transfer does not just lead to an economic development in the host state, but also to a knowledge transfer, with which personnel gets educated and trained by applying the knowledge, manufacturing goods or render services.[179]

All forms of intellectual property in copyrights, trademarks, patents, trade secrets, or other intangible creations can be *"transferred"* in two ways:[180]

– *Licensing of intellectual property*: A licensing agreement creates a contractual relationship between an intellectual property rights owner (licensor) and another who is authorized to use such rights for a limited period of time in exchange for an agreed payment (fee or royalty). There are various types of licenses like an exclusive license, sole license, non-exclusive license, knowledge license, software license, trademark license, cross license etc. However, license agreements are either one single contract or are part of a merger or acquisition transaction, a franchise, an investment agreement or part of a joint venture. Usually a licensing agreement contains reversionary rights which enable the licensor to get the transferred intellectual property rights back from the licensee once the license terminates (e.g., the agreement expires because of a fixed time period, the licensee breached the agreement or did not commercialize the work). Moreover, it is possible to license independently separate rights of intellectual property (e.g., it is possible to license separately each right of a copyright like the right to copy, the right to

---

[179]   See SORNARAJAH, International law, pp. 44-45.
[180]   See VAN LINDBERG, Intellectual property and open source: a practical guide to protecting code (2008), pp. 146 et seq.

distribute etc.). However, a license cannot last longer than the life of the intellectual property right (e.g., a license for a patent cannot extend beyond the life of patent protection).

– *Intellectual property assignment:* An intellectual property assignment is the permanent transfer of an owner's intellectual property rights from one party to another, often required to be written and signed. Such transfers occur either on their own or within a larger sale or purchase of assets. Furthermore, the assignment of intellectual property rights can be a viable business strategy if the transferors prefers to receive a substantial up-front payment (purchase price) instead of royalty payments throughout the commercialization period.

Either way, an investor has to be aware of the legislation of the home and the host state. Thus, an investor has not just to check the laws in the area where he wants to transfer the technology to but also the legislation in his home state for any restriction of such a transfer. For example, it is possible that the legislation has numerous statutory restrictions relating the export of technology (e.g., restrictions on export of technology with a primarily military use to an enemy, etc.). National acts may contain detailed restrictions in furtherance of state national security, foreign policy and short supply concerns. Sometimes an investor who wants to export technology has to obtain beforehand a clearance. Furthermore, some states require also that a cross border transfer of technology has to be registered. Moreover, competition law is also one of the subjects that has to be thought of whenever a technology transfer is prepared. Some states even offer tax incentives for a cross border transfer of technology. It is noteworthy that these *"technology transfer agreements"* can also be protected by BITs or MITs. Thus, in order to be sure of this, it is advisable to check the specific provisions of the BIT or MIT in question.[181]

---

[181] See CHRISTOPHER C. JOYNER, International law in the 21ˢᵗ century, Rules for global governance (2005), p. 271 and SORNARAJAH, International law, pp. 44-45.

VIII. Importance of the unification of commercial law for international trade and cross border investments

1. Generally

International trade and cross border investments have an important impact not just on the wealth of developed but also developing countries. Cross border transactions and investments require the conclusion of various contracts like the sale of goods, financing, transport etc. Nevertheless, contracts do not necessarily settle all issues. They may lead to disputes and finally to the resolution of them. Therefore, it is important for the parties to know their mutual rights and obligations. Thus, international agreements help to figure out the applicable law based on uniform commercial law texts and conventions.

2. Organizations/Commissions

There are four organizations/commissions, which try to facilitate international trade and cross border investments from a legal point of view:

— *United Nations Commission on International Trade Law (UNCITRAL)*: The United Nations Commission on International Trade Law (UNCITRAL) was established by the General Assembly in 1966 (Resolution 2205 (XXI) of December 17, 1966). In establishing the commission, the General Assembly recognized that disparities in national laws governing international trade created obstacles to the flow of trade, and it regarded the commission as the vehicle by which the United Nations could play a more active role in reducing or removing these obstacles.[182]

— *International Institute for the Unification of Private Law (UNIDROIT)*: The International Institute for the Unification of Private Law (UNIDROIT) is an independent intergovernmental Organisation with its seat in the Villa Aldobrandini in Rome. Its purpose is to

---

[182] See https://uncitral.un.org/en/about.

study needs and methods for modernizing, harmonizing and coordinating private and in particular commercial law as between states and groups of states and to formulate uniform law instruments, principles and rules to achieve those objectives.[183] Probably the most important result of the UNIDROIT's work are the UNIDROIT Principles of International Commercial Contracts that are often used in interpretation of international commercial contracts or sometimes even chosen by the parties as the law applicable to the contract.

– *Hague Conference on Private International Law (Hague Conference)*: The Hague Conference on private international law is an intergovernmental organization with the purpose *"to work for the progressive unification of the rules of private international law"* (Article 1 of the Statutes). Since 1951, the Conference adopted 38 international conventions, the practical operation of many of which is regularly reviewed by special commissions. Even when they are not ratified, the conventions have an influence upon legal systems, in both member and non-member states. They also form a source of inspiration for efforts to unify private international law at the regional level, for example within the Organization of American States or the European Union.[184]

– *World Trade Organization (WTO)*: The WTO is the only global trade organization[185] with the aim of setting the rules and principles for trade between nations. Although the addressees are not directly private parties, but states, its importance is in providing for fundamental principles for multilateral trade and thereby has major impact also on contracts between private parties.

---

[183] See https://www.unidroit.org/about-unidroit/overview.
[184] See https://www.hcch.net/en/about.
[185] As of end of 2018, it has 164 member states.

3. Conventions of importance for international trade and cross border business transactions

3.1. UN Convention on contracts for the international sale of goods (CISG)[186]

The United Nations Convention on Contracts for the International Sale of Goods (also called *"CISG"*) is a multilateral treaty that is a uniform international sales law, which has been prepared by UNCITRAL. The purpose of the CISG is to provide a modern, uniform and fair regime for contracts for the international sale of goods. As of the end of 2018, it has been ratified by 89 states that account for a significant proportion of world trade, making it one of the most successful international uniform laws. Initially it has been adopted by a diplomatic conference in 1980 and entered into force on January 1, 1988.

The contract of sale is the backbone of international trade in all countries, irrespective of their legal tradition or level of economic development. The CISG is therefore considered as one of the core international trade law conventions whose universal adoption is desirable.

The CISG is the result of a legislative effort that started at the beginning of the twentieth century. The resulting text provides a careful balance between the interests of the buyer and of the seller. It has also inspired contract law reforms at the national level.

The adoption of the CISG provides modern, uniform legislation for the international sale of goods that would apply whenever contracts for the sale of goods are concluded between parties with a place of business in contracting states. In these cases, the CISG would apply directly, avoiding recourse to rules of private international law to determine the law applicable to the contract, adding significantly to the certainty and predictability of international sales contracts.

Moreover, the CISG may apply to a contract for international sale of goods when the rules of private

---

[186] See http://www.uncitral.org/uncitral/en/uncitral_texts/sale_goods/1980CISG.html.

international law point at the law of a contracting state as the applicable one, or by virtue of the choice of the contractual parties, regardless of whether their places of business are located in a contracting state. In this latter case, the CISG provides a neutral body of rules that can be easily accepted in light of its transnational nature and of the wide availability of interpretative materials.

Finally, small and medium-sized enterprises as well as traders located in developing countries typically have reduced access to legal advice when negotiating a contract. Thus, they are more vulnerable to problems caused by inadequate treatment in the contract of issues relating to applicable law. The same enterprises and traders may also be the weaker contractual parties and could have difficulties in ensuring that the contractual balance is kept. Those merchants would therefore derive particular benefit from the default application of the fair and uniform regime of the CISG to contracts falling under its scope.

The CISG governs contracts for the international sales of goods between private businesses, excluding sales to consumers and sales of services, as well as sales of certain specified types of goods. Certain matters relating to the international sales of goods, for instance the validity of the contract and the effect of the contract on the property in the goods sold, fall outside the convention's scope. The second part of the CISG deals with the formation of the contract, which is concluded by the exchange of offer and acceptance. The third part of the CISG deals with the obligations of the parties to the contract. Obligations of the sellers include delivering goods in conformity with the quantity and quality stipulated in the contract, as well as related documents, and transferring the property in the goods. Obligations of the buyer include payment of the price and taking delivery of the goods. In addition, this part provides common rules regarding remedies for breach of the contract. The aggrieved party may require performance, claim damages or avoid the contract in case of fundamental breach. Additional rules regulate passing of risk, anticipatory breach of contract, damages, and exemption from performance of the contract. Finally, while the CISG allows for freedom of form of the contract, states may lodge a declaration requiring the written form.

The CISG applies only to international transactions and avoids the recourse to rules of private international law for those contracts falling under its scope of application. International contracts falling outside the scope of application of the CISG, as well as contracts subject to a valid choice of other law, would not be affected by the CISG. Purely domestic sale contracts are not affected by the CISG and remain regulated by domestic law.

3.2. Convention on the limitation period in the international sale of goods[187]

Convention on the Limitation Period in the International Sale of Goods (also *"Limitation Convention"*) is a uniform law treaty prepared by UNCITRAL, which deals with the prescription of actions relating to contracts for the international sale of goods due to the passage of time.

The Limitation Convention establishes uniform rules governing the period of time within which a party under a contract for the international sale of goods must commence legal proceedings against another party to assert a claim arising from the contract or relating to its breach, termination or validity. By doing so, it brings clarity and predictability on an aspect of great importance for the adjudication of the claim.

Most legal systems limit or prescribe a claim from being asserted after the lapse of a specified period of time to prevent the institution of legal proceedings at such a late date that the evidence relating to the claim is likely to be unreliable or lost and to protect against the uncertainty that would result if a party were to remain exposed to unasserted claims for an extensive period of time. However, numerous disparities exist among legal systems with respect to the conceptual basis for doing so, resulting in significant variations in the length of the limitation period and in the rules governing the claims after that period. Those differences may create difficulties in the enforcement of claims arising from international sales transactions. In

---

[187] See http://www.uncitral.org/uncitral/en/uncitral_texts/sale_goods/ 1974Convention_limitation_period.html.

response to those difficulties, the Limitation Convention was prepared and adopted in 1974. The Limitation Convention was further amended by a protocol adopted in 1980 in order to harmonize its text with that of the CISG, in particular, with regard to scope of application and admissible declarations. Indeed, the Limitation Convention may be functionally seen as a part of the CISG and, as such, considered as an important step towards a comprehensive standardization of international sales law.

The limitation period is set at four years (article 8 of the Limitation Convention). A limitation period of four years' duration was thought to accomplish the aims of the limitation period and yet to provide an adequate period of time to enable a party to an international sales contract to assert his claim against the other party. Subject to certain conditions, that period may be extended to a maximum of ten years (article 23 of the Limitation Convention). With respect to the time when the limitation period commences to run, the basic rule is that it commences on the date on which the claim accrues. The convention establishes when claims for breach of contract, for defects in the goods or other lack of conformity and for fraud are deemed to accrue. Furthermore, this convention also regulates certain questions pertaining to the effect of commencing proceedings in a contracting state.

The Limitation Convention further provides rules on the cessation and extension of the limitation period. The period ceases when the claimant commences judicial or arbitral proceedings or when it asserts claims in an existing process. If the proceedings end without a binding decision on the merits, it is deemed that the limitation period continued to run during the proceedings. However, if the period has expired during the proceedings or has less than one year to run, the claimant is granted an additional year to commence new proceedings (article 17 of the Limitation Convention).

No claim shall be recognized or enforced in legal proceedings commenced after the expiration of the limitation period (article 25(1) of the Limitation Convention). Such expiration is not to be taken into consideration unless invoked by parties to the proceedings (article 24 of the Limitation Convention). However, states can make a declaration allowing courts to take into account the expiration of the limitation period on their own initiative (article 36 of the Limitation Convention). Otherwise, the only exception to the rule barring recognition and enforcement occurs when the party raises its claim as a defense to or set-off against a claim asserted by the other party (article 25(2) of the Limitation Convention).

The Limitation Convention applies only to international transactions and avoids the recourse to rules of private international law for those contracts falling under its scope of application. International contracts falling outside the scope of application of the Limitation Convention, as well as contracts subject to a valid choice of other law, would not be affected by the Limitation Convention. Purely domestic sales contracts are not affected by the Limitation Convention and are regulated by domestic law.

IX.   Legal issues of joint ventures in developing countries

1.   Generally

A joint venture is a commercial arrangement between two or more independent parties in order to undertake economic activities together like developing and marketing products where the parties share risks, reduce costs and pool their resources, expertise, manufacturing know-how, marketing skills etc. to achieve a particular goal. Such joint ventures can be for one specific project only, or a continuing business relationship. They give each partner the opportunity to benefit significantly for the advantages of the other.[188] For example, in the oil and gas industry it is very common to form joint ventures.[189]

> **Example of a successful joint venture for manufacturing consumer electronics products in India**[190]
>
> A joint venture had brought together Indian and American partners to manufacture a specific consumer electronics product by a new legal entity in India. It was agreed that the Indian was responsible not only for manufacturing high-quality products, but also for marketing and distribution channel development, while the American partners supplied product and process technologies. The joint venture has been very successful and therefore the question of exporting these products came up. The partners would have to start to discuss whether exporting would meet their strategic goals and eventually how to proceed.

---

[188] See also FRÉDÉRIC PREVOT/PIERRE-XAVIER MESCHI, Evolution of an international joint venture: the case of a French – Brazilian joint venture, in: Thunderbird International Business Review, Vol. 48(3) (2006), pp. 297 et seq.

[189] See UNITED NATIONS CONFERENCE ON TRADE AND DEVELOPMENT, Word investment report 2007, Transnational corporations, extractive industries and development (2007), p. 159.

[190] ROBERT MILLER/JACK GLEN/FRED JASPERSEN/YANNIS KARMOKOLIAS, International joint ventures in developing countries, in: Finance & Development (March 1997), p. 28.

2.   Types of joint ventures

There are the following types of joint ventures:

2.1.   Contractual joint venture

Contractual joint ventures are joint business undertakings based on an agreement between two or more natural persons or legal entities who combine their efforts and resources in order to achieve some specific goal without establishing a separate legal entity. Usually, such agreements are made for short- to medium term alliances or for time-limited projects (e.g., in the field of civil engineering, and the construction, building and equipment supply industries).[191]

2.2.   Equity joint venture

An equity joint venture is based on an agreement between two or more natural persons or legal entities to enter for a long-term duration into a separate business venture together. The business structure for an equity joint venture is a separate legal entity, which is usually incorporated in the host state.[192]

3.   Reasons for a joint venture

Some countries require foreign investors to form joint ventures with domestic legal entities or natural persons in order to enter the domestic market in the host state. In some jurisdictions, joint ventures must take a certain form. In other jurisdictions, joint ventures may be organized in accordance with a range of different structures. For example, Brazilian legislation has not expressly regulated joint

---

[191] Contractual joint ventures are often also called cooperative joint ventures or non-corporate joint ventures. See YADONG LUO, Multinational enterprises in emerging markets (2002), p. 215 and KARL F. KREUZER, Legal aspects of international joint ventures in agriculture, pp. 2-3 and 8.

[192] See KREUZER, op. cit., pp. 2-3 and 6-7.

ventures and thus not established a special treatment for this kind of arrangements. However, Brazilian law provides for several forms of business organizations, such as general partnerships, limited partnerships, limited companies and joint stock companies. Moreover, parties incorporating a joint venture company usually execute a shareholders' or a quotaholders' agreement (depending on the form of business organization being incorporated).[193]

The requirement to set up a legal entity in the host state has in principle[194] not to be seen negatively as the establishment of a joint venture offers advantages to both the investor and the host state:[195]

The principal advantages for the investor are:
1. Safeguarding or expanding of markets (instead of exports);
2. Risk sharing (the investor can share costs associated with marketing, product development, and other expenses, and thus reducing the financial burden);
3. Security of supply (raw materials);
4. Local marketing know-how;
5. Contacts with local banks and public authorities;
6. In certain political, social or economic circumstances it may be the only way to invest in a foreign country, gain new markets or defend or expand acquired markets;
7. Sharing of capital costs; and
8. Low labor and transport costs.

---

[193] See GUILHERME LEITE/TALITA ALVES RODRIGUES, Brazil, in: International joint ventures, the comparative law yearbook of international business, Special issue, edited by Dennis Campbell (2008), pp. 3-4.

[194] However, any special requirements for foreign investments like the necessity that in order to make the investment the foreign investor has to set up a particular legal form, is a restriction on the party autonomy and thus an exception to this basic legal principle.

[195] See AIMIN YAN/YADONG LUO, International joint ventures, theory and practice (2001), pp. 112-113 and MAMARINTA P. MABABYA, The role of multinational companies in the middle east: the case of Saudi Arabia (2002), pp. 179-180 and the list made by KREUZER, op. cit., pp. 5-6.

The principal advantages for the home state are:

1. Foreign exchange earnings through capital import and commodity export;
2. Acquisition of new technology (a joint venture allows very often an access to new technology; sharing innovative and proprietary technology can improve products, as well as the understanding of technological processes);
3. Acquisition of technical skills;
4. Acquisition of management know-how;
5. Import substitution;
6. Creation of employment; and
7. Utilization and processing of local resources for export.

4. Joint venture agreement

4.1. Generally

Regardless of the type of joint venture, which has been chosen by the parties, and the fact that there is no limit to the matters that can be covered in a joint venture agreement, a clear agreement is essential for building a good relationship. Thus, the parties should consider including at least the following points in a joint venture agreement.[196]

4.2. Definitions

It is common to start such agreements with the definitions. They usually cover the parties etc.

---

[196] See for example also the checklist for a model joint venture agreement by the American Bar Association (https://apps.americanbar.org/ buslaw/newsletter/0049/materials/book.pdf) and ALAN S. GUTTERMAN, A short course in international joint ventures, how to negotiate, establish and manage an international joint venture (2009), pp. 13 et seq.

4.3. Objective of the joint venture

A joint venture agreement should include a section at the beginning covering the scope/purpose of the joint venture. Not only is this sometimes a matter of local law, but it is often essential to make sure both parties are clear on the scope and scale of the joint venture's operations. This will help when the agreement and the genuine will of the parties have to be interpreted, which may be important in case of a dispute. Thus, it has to be held what activities the joint venture does expressly intend to do.

4.4. Contributions of the parties

The parties usually list their contributions (and the liability for the contributions) regarding the joint venture.

Possible contributions of a foreign investor are:
– technical skills and know how,
– patents,
– marketing techniques,
– production techniques,
– specialized personnel, and/or
– financial resources.

Possible contributions of a domestic partner are:
– real estate,
– existing production facilities,
– capital,
– environmental knowledge,
– supplier, labour, customer contacts, and/or
– social and political goodwill.

4.5. Organization and management of the joint venture

The agreement has to address what kind of organization will be formed. If it is necessary to use a corporate vehicle for the joint venture, then the joint venture agreement should define the form of the legal entity. The joint ventures' governance structure will depend largely on the actual structure chosen.

4.6. New parties

The agreement has to contain clauses, which explain how will be dealt with possible new partners. Usually new partners are just allowed when both parties accept the new partners. Furthermore, such agreements contain requirements/prohibitions regarding the sale of the shares or quotas of the joint venture legal entity.

4.7. Termination of the joint venture

The termination provisions for a joint venture belong to the most important terms of the entire document. The agreement would typically provide for termination due to a breach of the agreement by the other party, or if one of the parties goes into bankruptcy, or if there is a change of control of one of the parties. The termination provisions might also cover the termination of the joint venture in the event of expropriation of the joint venture's assets.

4.8. Choice of law-clause

Many national jurisdictions allow the parties of a joint venture to choose the applicable law to their contractual relationship. Thus, it is important that the parties to a joint venture agreement choose and specify the governing law.

4.9. Dispute resolution mechanism

The agreement should contain clauses, with which the parties choose a dispute resolution mechanism (e.g., arbitration proceedings shall be conducted under the rules of UNCITRAL etc.).

5.   Tax issues

Very often tax issues that arise from the establishment, operation and termination of a joint venture have an impact on the choice between the aforementioned types of vehicles. Thus, it is important that either the foreign investor as well as the joint venture partner in the host state verify the respective taxation in each state. It is noteworthy that some states give unilateral tax reductions/exemptions for joint ventures. Furthermore, the parties of a joint venture should also consult the BITs, MITs or double taxation agreements in order to avoid double taxation issues.[198]

6.   Competition law issues

In principle, cooperation of undertakings, in spite of their positive effects, might raise concerns of competition

---

[197] See MYLES MCCORMICK/DAVID SHEPPARD, Egypt to pay Spanish-Italian JV $2bn in natural gas dispute, in: Financial Times (September 3, 2018).
[198] See GUTTERMAN, Joint Ventures, p. 20.

authorities since such a cooperation could increase the risk of anticompetitive behavior of the undertakings concerned; instead of competing between themselves, which would be a logical and natural behavior on the market, undertakings become business partners and consequently are not competitors. This might ultimately be detrimental for consumers. Whether there really are competition concerns resulting from a particular joint venture shall depend on all the circumstances of the case, but these issues should never be neglected.

X. Legal aspects of privatization in developing countries

1. Generally

Privatization is a tool which enables the private sector to provide services in order to achieve public objectives and thus aims to make sure that those services are provided as effectively and as efficiently as possible.[199] Many developing countries received substantial foreign investments through privatization of important sectors of the local economy and infrastructure (e.g., in the telecommunication sector, public transportation). Thus, privatization is the process of a full or partial transfer of ownership from the public to the private sector. Therefore, it is somehow the reverse process of nationalization.[200] Sometimes, it is also an opening of state monopolies to private competition, i.e., the citizen have a wider choice at a competitive price. However, there have been also governmental services such as health and education, which have been target of privatization in many countries and increasingly negative voices argued that entrusting the private sector with the control of important services reduces the governments' control over them and leads to excessive cost cutting and finally to poor quality service. Furthermore, privatization can be accompanied by corruption as the local government might award contracts or concession to investors of their choosing without allowing third parties to make a bid.

In general, privatization was common during the immediate post-World War II period. However, in the former colonies due to the de-colonialization the opposite happened. Setting

---

[199] See STUART BUTLER, Privatization for public purposes, in: Privatization and its alternatives, edited by William T. Gromley, Jr. (1991), p. 26.
[200] See CARL B. GREENIDGE, Privatization in Ghana, in: Privatization, a global perspective, edited by V. V. Ramanadham (1993), p. 184; BALU L. BUMB, Privatization of agribusiness input markets, in: Privatization and deregulation, needed policy reforms for agribusiness development, edited by Surjit S. Sidhu/Mohinder S. Mudahar (1999), p. 67 and T. MAKONDO, Privatisation as a major reform in public sector management, in: Public finance fundamentals, edited by Kabelo Moeti et al. (2007), p. 115.

up state-owned enterprises was a response in getting independent from the former colonial powers as there were no local privately owned legal entities, which were able to take over the local businesses. However, privatization became a more dominant economic trend since the 1980s and 1990s and was part of a *"global wave"* of neo liberal policies.[201] Also in 1990s there was following the Perestroika policy of Mikhail Gorbachev a massive privatization of the formerly centrally planned and government-owned companies.[202] Nowadays in Latin America, some parts of Asia and Africa, privatization is associated with re-adjusting the structures (structure adjustment programs), because many countries were on the edge of bankruptcy and the IMF/World Bank was willing to give money under the condition of implementing structure adjustment programs.

2.   Forms of Privatization

There are various forms of privatization like the following:

2.1.   Contracting out

Contracting out is the simplest form of privatization and thus widely used. It is the use of privately held legal entities to provide public services. Nevertheless, the government remains in charge of the activities by controlling their performance with the idea of ensuring that they are of the appropriate quality and available to all citizens. Due to this outsourcing there is a shift of the jobs and services from the public to the private sector. This type of privatization gives greater flexibility to the government by not having to keep a costly function in-house. However, the use of exclusive contracts should be avoided if possible as one of the virtues of privatization is to allow competition to take place and this

---

[201] See NICOLAS VAN DE WALLE, Privatization in developing countries: a review of the issues, in: World Development, Vol. 17, No. 5 (1989), p. 601.

[202] See International Labour Organization, sectoral activities programme, terms of employment and working conditions in health sector reforms, JMHSR/1998, p. 15.

is accomplished by an open door policy to all entrepreneurs in the private sector.[203]

2.2.   Voucher privatization

Voucher privatization is a method where citizens get or can inexpensively buy vouchers of potential shares in any state-owned company. This form of privatization has mainly been used in the early to mid-1990s in countries like Russia, Bulgaria, Slovenia and Czechoslovakia.[204]

2.3.   Sale of shares or assets of a state-owned legal entity

Another method of privatization is the sale of the majority or all of the shares of a before fully state-owned legal entity. However, it is also possible to sell the assets of an entire state-owned legal entity (or part of it) to a foreign investor. Usually it is advisable to choose the investor by the issuance of a tender in a transparent procedure. The host state advertises that it wants to privatize a sector (e.g., telecommunications), and that bids have to be made to the government (e.g., submission day is xx.xx 2019). For example, UNCITRAL has a Model Law on Public Procurement, which explains such a procedure.[205]

2.4.   Concessions

The government gives a concession to a legal entity to render a service or run a business on the property of the state

---

[203] JACQUES V. DINAVO, Privatization in developing countries, its impact on economic development and democracy (1995), pp. 6-7 and BUTLER, op. cit., pp. 21 et seq.

[204] See BUTLER, op. cit., pp. 23-24; MARC HOLZER/BYRON E. PRICE/ HWANG-SUN KANG, Public productivity handbook, edited by Marc Holzer/Seok-Hwan Lee (2004), p. 89.

[205] See HOLZER/ PRICE/KANG, op. cit., p. 91.

for a specific period of time, for which the concession holder has to pay royalties (e.g., BOTs).[206]

3. Reasons for privatization

There was in the past a *"push"* towards privatization, especially due to expectations of the government to lose less money with its state-owned legal entities and to be more efficient.[207] However, there have been counterexamples which showed that state-owned companies are doing equally well or even better than the privately owned.[208]

There are various reasons for privatization:[209]

- *Infrastructure problems*: Most of the state-owned legal entities performed poorly. They often did not provide the desired basic infrastructure.
- *Competition:* The private sector is more efficient and thus there is a widespread believe that private managers can deliver at lower costs services similar or superior to those of public managers. However, state-owned legal entities have – as there is no competition – little incentive to reduce costs and improve efficiency.
- *Less corruption:* There is the opinion that the public sector is more exposed to corruption than the private sector.
- *Shareholder control:* Several shareholders can check better what is happening in the legal entities. However, in state-owned legal entities there is just one *"shareholder"* and thus less control.

---

[206] See MAKONDO, op. cit., p. 115.
[207] PAUL COOK, Private sector development strategy in developing countries, in: Privatization and market development, global movements in public policy ideas, edited by Graeme Hodge (2006), p. 90.
[208] For example, in Sweden many state-owned legal companies were made efficient and profitable by the introduction of an incentive scheme that let these companies operate equally good or better than any private competitor, see RALPH T. NIEMEYER, Germany after capitalism (2012), p. 74.
[209] HOLZER, op. cit., pp. 92-93; BUMB, op. cit., pp. 69-70 and DINAVO, op. cit., pp. 10 et seq.

- *Access to technology:* A government is often not able to *"catch up"* with or to obtain the newest technology.
- *"Fiscal Tool":* Privatization is also seen as a fiscal tool as most privatization programs are considered as a fiscal relief by cutting government subsidies to money-losing state-owned legal entities.

4.   Financing of infrastructure projects

The financing of infrastructure projects in developing countries is capital-intensive and has a long-term focus. Very often a foreign investor, a consortium of investors and other participants like the government, private individuals or legal entities of the host state come together in order to realize infrastructure projects that would be usually too big for individual investors or where governments face budgetary constraints. The investors are repaid only from the cash flow generated by the project or, in the event of complete failure, from the value of the project's assets.[210]

Especially, in the last fifty years the Build Operate Transfer-structures (BOT) have become more and more frequently used to finance the construction of highways, bridges, power plants, railroads, ports and airports in order to outsource public projects by the government to the private sector.[211] Under a BOT, a government typically grants a concession for a specified period (usually 10 to 30 years) to an investor or a consortium of investors under which the project company has the right to build and operate itself or through a third party a public infrastructure project. The government retains ownership of the facility and becomes both the customer and the regulator of the service. Should the state choose to take over the facility/infrastructure earlier than the agreed concession period, then the investor or consortium of

---

[210] See ASHOKA MODY, in: Infrastructure delivery: new ideas, big gains, no panaceas, in: Infrastructure delivery, private initiative and the public good, edited by Ashoka Mody (1996), p. xxxi and WORLD DEVELOPMENT REPORT 1994, Infrastructure for development (1994), p. 94.

[211] See FREDERICK PRETORIUS/PAUL LEJOT/ARTHUR MCINNIS/DOUGLAS ARNER/BERRY FONG-CHUNG HSU, Project finance for construction and infrastructure, principles and case studies (2008), pp. 12-13.

investors has to be financially compensated for their investments.[212]

Besides the aforementioned BOTs, there are various different types of such project financing like:[213]

- ROT: rehabilitate, operate, transfer;
- BOOT: build, operate, own, transfer;
- BLT: build, lease, transfer;
- BT: build, transfer;
- MOT: modernize, operate, transfer; and
- DOT: develop, operate, transfer.

Regardless of these different types, the concept is always the same. Money from the private sector is used to finance public infrastructure.

In the old concession systems, the state gave up its rights and along with it land or a mine to a private investor for free exploitation. However, nowadays in BOTs, the state decides what kind of infrastructure it needs (e.g., ports, railroads etc.) and thus, the investor or the consortium of investors has

---

[212] See MIRJAM BULT-SPIERING/GEERT DEWULF, Strategic issues in public-private partnerships, an internal perspective (2006), p. 6.
[213] See TONY MERNA/CYRUS NJIRU, Financing infrastructure projects (2002), p. 90; SALACUSE, The three laws of international investment, p. 220 and ESTEBAN C. BULJEVICH/YOON S. PARK, Project financing and the international financial markets (1999), p. 117.

to tailor the project to the wishes of the state. The investors are selected through bidding or other evaluative processes.

XI.   International efforts against corruption

1.   Generally

There is hardly any state in the world in which the people involved in foreign investments are immune to corruption[214]. Corruption is an abuse of entrusted power for private gain and reduces access to public services by diverting public resources for private gain.[215] Even the most perfect legislation is not able entirely to prevent corruption as it is part of the human nature. Unfortunately, such corruption undermines also human and economic development and it strikes at the heart of democracy by corroding rule of law, democratic institutions and public trust in leaders. For the poor, women and minorities, corruption means even less access to jobs, justice or any fair and equal opportunity.[216]

Examples of corruption in relation with foreign investments[217]		
Date	Legal Entity	Case
12/15/2008	Siemens (Germany)	Bribed Argentine government officials to win government contract

---

[214] It is also worth mentioning that the world arbitration practice clearly demonstrates that investments which are not made in good faith or which are made by use of, *inter alia,* corruption do not enjoy legal protection. Thus, it is not only that corruption is in general perceived as utterly detrimental for society, it is legally also considered as being incompatible with the mere definition of investments; such "investments" which are made by use of corruption do not satisfy the essential element of investments which have to be legal.

[215] LUKMAN HAREES, The mirage of dignity on the highways of humans 'progress': - the bystanders' perspective (2012), p. 488.

[216] UNDP TANZANIA SUCCESS STORIES, FIGHTING CORRUPTION (2013), p. 1.

[217] See MERRILL GOOZNER, The ten largest global business corruption cases, December 13, 2011, in: The Fiscal Times (http://www.thefiscaltimes.com/Articles/2011/12/13/The-Ten-Largest-Global-Business-Corruption-Cases).

2/11/2009	KBR/Halliburton (USA)	Four-company global consortium bribed Nigerian officials to win construction contracts
4/1/2010	Daimler AG (Germany)	Made illegal payments to foreign officials worth tens of millions of dollars in at least 22 countries
11/4/2010	Panalpina World Transport (Switzerland)	Oil transport company and United States affiliate paid thousands of bribes totaling at least $27 million to foreign officials in at least seven countries, including Angola, Azerbaijan, Brazil, Kazakhstan, Nigeria, Russia and Turkmenistan

2.   Instruments

Many states nowadays have an anti-corruption legislation. However, these states had competitive problems in comparison with other states that had no such legislation. Thus, the more developed countries rallied in international forums for international conventions against corruption:

2.1.   United Nations Convention against Corruption (UNCAC)

The United Nations Convention against Corruption (UNCAC) is a multilateral convention negotiated by members of the United Nations. It is the first global legally binding international anti-corruption instrument. It entered into force in 2005 and has 186 parties. The first part of the convention deals with the prevention of corruption – the possible measures against it. The second part of the convention refers to criminal law enforcement – countries have to establish criminal codes etc. The third part deals with asset recovery. The last part is about international cooperation.

2.2. Inter-American Convention Against Corruption (OAS Convention)

This Convention was adopted in 1996 by the member nations of the Organization of American States (OAS) and thus it is a regional instrument. This convention made extraterritorial bribery of government officials illegal and convention required their signatories to pass domestic implementing legislation.

2.3. Convention on Combating Bribery in International Business Transactions (OECD Anti-Bribery Convention)

This convention made extraterritorial bribery of government officials illegal and convention required their signatories to pass domestic implementing legislation. Signatory states are required to put in place legislation that criminalizes the act of bribing a foreign public official. The OECD has no authority to implement the convention, but instead monitors implementation by participating countries. Countries are responsible for implementing laws and regulations that conform to the convention and therefore provide for enforcement.

2.4. African Union Convention on Preventing and Combating Corruption

The African Union Convention on Preventing and Combating Corruption was adopted in 2003 to fight rampant political corruption on the African continent. It represents regional consensus on what African States should do in the areas of prevention, criminalization, international cooperation and asset recovery. The convention covers a wide range of offences including bribery (domestic or foreign), diversion of property by public officials, trading in influence, illicit enrichment, money laundering and concealment of property and primarily consists of mandatory provisions.

2.5. WTO Agreement on Government Procurement

The aim of the agreement is to open up, as much as possible, government procurement markets to international competition and to help eradicate corruption in this sector. Therefore, the WTO requires member states to enact legislation to punish corruption.

2.6. United Nations Resolution Against Corruption and Bribery International Commercial Transaction

This UN resolution from 1996 urges members to criminalize the payment of bribes to public office holders of other States in international commercial transactions and encourages members to establish programs to deter and prevent bribery and corruption.

2.7. United Nations International Code of Conduct of Public Officials

On December 12, 1996, the UN General Assembly adopted this non-binding code, which encouraged states to monitor the acts of officials and to prevent corruption.

2.8. Council of Europe's (Council's) Criminal Law Convention on Corruption

The Council of Europe's (Council's) Criminal Law Convention on Corruption, which entered into force in 2002, criminalizes bribes paid to public officials and private parties, as well as a wide range of other criminal offenses connected with corruption.

2.9. European Union's Convention on the Fight Against Corruption involving Officials of the European Communities or Officials of Member States of the European

This convention was adopted on May 26, 1997, and it criminalizes the bribery of EU officials as well as public officials of EU member states. However, it does not address transnational bribery with foreign officials that are not members of the European Union.

2.10. United Nations Global Compact (UN Global Compact)

The United Nations Global Compact is a United Nations initiative to encourage businesses worldwide to adopt sustainable and socially responsible policies, and to report on their implementation. The UN Global Compact is a principle-based framework for businesses, stating ten principles in the areas of human rights, labor, the environment and anti-corruption. Principle 10 states that businesses should work against corruption in all its forms, including extortion and bribery. It is important to note that the UN Global Compact is not a regulatory instrument, but rather a forum for discussion and a network for communication including governments, companies and labor organizations, whose actions it seeks to influence, and civil society organizations, representing its stakeholders.

2.11. Financial Action Task Force (on Money Laundering) (FATF)

The Financial Action Task Force (on Money Laundering) (FATF), also known by its French name *"Groupe d'action financière (GAFI)"*, is an intergovernmental organization founded in 1989 on the initiative of the G7 to develop policies to combat money laundering. In 2001 the purpose expanded to act on terrorism financing. In addition, the FATF attaches a great importance to the fight against corruption as corruption has the potential to bring

144

catastrophic harm to economic development, the fight against organized crime, and respect for the law and effective governance.

XII. Corporate social responsibility (CSR) and international investments

1. Generally

Corporate social responsibility (CSR) in relation to international investments can be defined as the contribution made by foreign investors with their investments in order to achieve a sustainable development in host states. Taking into account CSR issues like working conditions, human rights, environment, anti-corruption measures, fair competition, consumer interests, taxes, transparency, gender equality etc. does not just support and improve a sustainable development or maximize the positive societal outcome of investments as well as business activities in the host state, but also help to achieve a bigger economic growth and a safer investment environment with a lower risk of nationalizations.

Various BITs and MITs reflect CSR issues. It is noteworthy that the inclusion of CSR concepts and principles in trade and investment agreements are considered to present an opportunity for achieving greater coherence in CSR by providing signals to companies about which guidelines, standards and labels to adopt. For example, some of these agreements provide for the establishment of a committee on investments that will host a forum to promote co-operation and facilitate joint initiatives on CSR. This type of formal networks help to promote CSR coherence.

Canada - Peru Free Trade Agreement
Chapter Eight - Investment
Section A- Substantive Obligations

Article 809: Health, Safety and Environmental Measures

The Parties recognize that it is inappropriate to encourage investment by relaxing domestic health, safety or environmental measures. Accordingly, a Party should not waive or otherwise derogate from, or offer to waive or otherwise derogate from, such measures as an encouragement for the establishment, acquisition, expansion or retention in its territory of an investment of an investor.

146

If a Party considers that the other Party has offered such an encouragement, it may request consultations with the other Party and the two Parties shall consult with a view to avoiding any such encouragement.

Article 810: Corporate Social Responsibility

Each Party should encourage enterprises operating within its territory or subject to its jurisdiction to voluntarily incorporate internationally recognized standards of corporate social responsibility in their internal policies, such as statements of principle that have been endorsed or are supported by the Parties. These principles address issues such as labor, the environment, human rights, community relations and anti-corruption. The Parties remind those enterprises of the importance of incorporating such corporate social responsibility standards in their internal policies.

Article 817: Committee on Investment

The Parties hereby establish a Committee on Investment, comprising representatives of each Party.

The Committee shall provide a forum for the Parties to consult on issues related to this Chapter that are referred to it by a Party. The Committee shall meet at such times as agreed by the Parties and should work to promote cooperation and facilitate joint initiatives, which may address issues such as corporate social responsibility and investment facilitation.

Furthermore, not just host states, but also the home states of foreign investors enacted national legislations which force a foreign investor to take CSR issues into account for its investment in a host state.

2.   Benefits of CSR[218]

For example, foreign investors benefit from taking into account CSR issues as follows:

–   By making savings in energy and raw material consumption thanks to more productive workers (e.g. reducing illness- and accident-related absences and early retirement from working life), better credit terms and easier access to the capital market, foreign investors benefit financially from CSR. A consistent CSR management can help foreign investors to obtain a favorable market position, can boost innovation and avoid reputational threats.
–   Respecting CSR can have a positive influence for foreign investors as customers are increasingly taking CSR criteria into account.
–   A reputation as a responsible employer also boosts recruitment and motivates employees.
–   A responsible business conduct can give foreign investors an advantage in public tenders as more and more governments of the host states require strict adherence to law provisions regarding employment conditions and equal pay.

Foreign investments which take CSR issues into account can provide for the following positive societal outcome:

–   Consistent and broad implementation of CSR do not just help to overcome social challenges in the host state (e.g., skills shortage, unemployment, balancing work and family), but also position the home state of the investor as a responsible economy.
–   Respecting CSR issues helps to preserve natural resources, protect health and improve life quality.
–   Many countries do not have adequate statutory provisions or do not implement these adequately, despite being responsible for developing and implementing the framework conditions for their own social and economic policies. If an investor reduces the social and

---

[218]   See https://www.seco.admin.ch/seco/en/home/Aussenwirtschafts
politik_Wirtschaftliche_Zusammenarbeit/Wirtschaftsbeziehungen/
Gesellschaftliche_Verantwortung_der_Unternehmen/Nutzen_der_
CSR1.html.

environmental risks in the host state, then this does not just improve the living conditions, but also the global sustainability.

3. International CSR standards

3.1. Generally

Recently, CSR has become more and more important on the international stage and undergone conceptual changes. New tools have been developed and existing ones updated and enhanced. After the ISO 26000 Guidance on social responsibility was published in 2010, the updated OECD Declaration on international investment and multinational enterprises and the UN Guiding Principles on Business and Human Rights were released in 2011. The UN Sustainable Development Goals of the 2030 Agenda for Sustainable Development, which appeared in 2015, also emphasize the contribution the private sector can make to sustainable development.

3.2. OECD Declaration on international investment and multinational enterprises

The OECD works to enhance the contribution of international investment to growth and sustainable development worldwide by advancing investment policy reform and international co-operation. First adopted in 1976, the OECD Declaration on international investment and multinational enterprises is a policy commitment by adhering governments to provide an open and transparent environment for international investments and to encourage the positive contribution multinational enterprises can make to economic and social progress. All parts of the Declaration are subject to periodical reviews. The most recent review, which was completed in May 2011, concerned the Guidelines for Multinational Enterprises. All 36 OECD countries, and 12 non-OECD countries[219] have subscribed to the Declaration.

The Declaration consists of four elements:

- *Guidelines for Multinational Enterprises*: The Guidelines for Multinational Enterprises[220] are recommendations on responsible business conduct addressed by governments to multinational enterprises operating in or from adhering countries. Observance of the Guidelines is supported by a unique implementation mechanism: adhering governments – through their network of National Contact Points (NCP) [221] – are responsible for promoting the Guidelines and helping to resolve issues that arise under the specific instances procedures. Any suspected breach against the OECD guidelines can be reported to the NCPs, which offer a platform for dialogue or a mediation procedure. Sector-specific guidelines (covering minerals, agriculture, textiles, finance, etc.)[222] support implementation of the OECD guidelines and enterprises' due diligence in particular.
- *National Treatment*: A voluntary undertaking by adhering countries to accord to foreign-controlled enterprises on their territories treatment no less favourable than that accorded in like situations to domestic enterprises.
- *Conflicting requirements*: Adhering countries shall co-operate in order to avoid or minimize the imposition of conflicting requirements on multinational enterprises.
- *International investment incentives and disincentives*: adhering countries recognise the need to give due weight to the interest of adhering countries affected by laws and practices in this field; they will endeavour to make measures as transparent as possible.

---

[219] Argentina, Brazil, Colombia, Costa Rica, Egypt, Jordan, Kazakhstan, Morocco, Peru, Romania, Tunisia and Ukraine.
[220] See http://mneguidelines.oecd.org/.
[221] See http://mneguidelines.oecd.org/ncps/.
[222] See http://mneguidelines.oecd.org/sectors/.

3.3. UN Guiding Principles on Business and Human Rights

The UN Guiding Principles on Business and Human Rights[223] include 31 principles and are based on three pillars:
- *State duty to protect human rights*: Countries must take the necessary measures (e.g., laws, incentives and awareness raising) in order to protect the population from human rights abuses.
- *Corporate responsibility*: Legal entities must act with due diligence in order to avoid infringing the rights of others and to address any negative impacts. The UN principles hold that legal entities have the power to affect all of the internationally recognized rights. Thus, there is a responsibility of both the state and the private sector to acknowledge their respective roles in upholding and protecting human rights.
- *Access to remedy*: Countries and legal entities have a responsibility to facilitate effective remediation for those affected by means of judicial and extrajudicial measures.

The principles can be applied to all countries and legal entities regardless of their size, sector, location or ownership and organizational structures. However, they do not constitute international obligations.

3.4. UN Global Compact

Launched in 2000, the United Nations Global Compact (UNGC)[224] is a call to legal entities to align strategies and operations with universal principles on human rights, labor, environment and anti-corruption, and take actions that advance societal goals. Today, many hundreds of companies and non-profit organizations from all regions of the world, are engaged in the UN Global Compact, working to advance 10 Universal Principles in the areas of human rights, labor, the environment and anti-corruption.

---

[223] See https://www.ohchr.org/Documents/Publications/GuidingPrinciples BusinessHR_EN.pdf.
[224] See https://www.globalcompact.ch/ungc.

THE 10 PRINCIPLES:

HUMAN RIGHTS

1. Businesses should support and respect the protection of internationally proclaimed human rights; and
2. Make sure that they are not complicit in human rights abuses.

LABOR

3. Businesses should uphold the freedom of association and the effective recognition of the right to collective bargaining;
4. The elimination of all forms of forced and compulsory labor;
5. The effective abolition of child labor; and
6. The elimination of discrimination in respect of employment and occupation.

ENVIRONMENT

7. Businesses should support a precautionary approach to environmental challenges;
8. Undertake initiatives to promote greater environmental responsibility; and
9. Encourage the development and diffusion of environmentally friendly technologies.

ANTI-CORRUPTION

10. Businesses should work against all forms of corruption, including extortion and bribery.

Once a signatory to the UN Global Compact, organizations are expected to:

− set in motion changes to their operations in order to implement the 10 principles;
− publicly advocate the Global Compact and its principles via communications vehicles such as press releases, speeches, etc.;
− business participants must publish an annual Communication on Progress (COP) that describes the ways in which the business supports the Global Compact and its 10 principles; and

152

– non business participants must publish an annual Communication on Engagement (COE) that describes the ways in which the organization supports the Global Compact and its 10 principles,

3.5. ISO 26000 Guidance on Social Responsibility

ISO 26000 – Guidance on social responsibility[225] provides guidance to all types of businesses and organizations, regardless of their size or location, on:

– concepts, terms and definitions related to social responsibility;
– the background, trends and characteristics of social responsibility;
– principles and practices relating to social responsibility;
– the core subjects and issues of social responsibility;
– integrating, implementing and promoting socially responsible behavior throughout the organization and, through its policies and practices, within its sphere of influence;
– identifying and engaging with stakeholders; and
– communicating commitments, performance and other information related to social responsibility.

ISO 26000 – Guidance on social responsibility is intended to assist businesses and organizations in contributing to sustainable development. It is intended to encourage them to go beyond legal compliance, recognizing that compliance with law is a fundamental duty of any organization and an essential part of their social responsibility. It is intended to promote common understanding in the field of social responsibility, and to complement other instruments and initiatives for social responsibility, not to replace them.

3.6. Global Reporting Initiative

The Global Reporting Initiative (GRI)[226] helps businesses and governments worldwide to understand and communicate

---

[225] See https://www.iso.org/iso-26000-social-responsibility.html.

their impact on critical sustainability issues such as climate change, human rights, governance and social well-being. This enables real action to create social, environmental and economic benefits for everyone. The GRI Sustainability Reporting Standards are developed with true multi-stakeholder contributions and rooted in the public interest.

4.   International CSR developments

4.1.   2030 Agenda for Sustainable Development (UN development goals)[227]

The 2030 Agenda for Sustainable Development (UN development goals)[228] was developed by the international community in 2015 in order to contribute to global development, promote human well-being and to protect the environment. The 17 Sustainable Development Goals and their 169 targets form a core element of this agenda.

4.2.   EU Strategy (2011-14) for Corporate Social Responsibility[229]

The EU Strategy (2011–14) for Corporate Social Responsibility describes the EU's strategic approach and the specific measures it has in place regarding CSR. The European Commission believes that CSR is important for the sustainability, competitiveness, and innovation of EU enterprises and the EU economy. It brings benefits for risk management, cost savings, access to capital, customer relationships, and human resource management.

---

[226] See https://www.globalreporting.org.
[227] See
https://sustainabledevelopment.un.org/post2015/transformingourworld.
[228] See
https://sustainabledevelopment.un.org/post2015/transformingourworld.
[229] See http://ec.europa.eu/growth/industry/corporate-social-responsibility/.

Made in the USA
Middletown, DE
06 November 2022

14267510R00106